EYEWITNESS TRAVEL

PHRASE BOOK

ITALIAN

REVISED EDITION

DK LONDON

Senior Editor Christine Stroyan
Senior Art Editors Anna Hall, Amy Child
Art Director Karen Self
Associate Publisher Liz Wheeler
Publishing Director Jonathan Metcalf
Proofreading Margherita Doré, in association with
First Edition Translations Ltd, Cambridge, UK
Senior Pre-Producer Andy Hilliard
Senior Producers Gary Batchelor, Anna Vallarino

DK DELHI

Assistant Editor Sugandha Agarwal
Assistant Art Editor
Anukriti Arora
Art Editors Ravi Indiver,
Mansi Agarwal
Senior Art Editor Chhaya Sajwan
Managing Editor Soma B. Chowdhury
Senior Managing Art Editor
Arunesh Talapatra

Production Manager Pankaj Sharma
Preproduction Managers
Sunil Sharma, Balwant Singh
Senior DTP Designers
Tarun Sharma, Shanker Prasad,
Neeraj Bhatia, Ajay Verma

First published in Great Britain in 2008
This revised edition published in 2017 by
Dorling Kindersley Limited,
80 Strand, London WC2R 0RL
A Penguin Random House Company

Copyright © 2008, 2017 Dorling Kindersley Ltd
10 9 8 7 6 5 4 3 2 1
001–300208–Jun/17

A CIP catalogue record for this book is available from the British Library

ISBN: 978-0-2412-8938-9

Printed and bound in China

A WORLD OF IDEAS:
SEE ALL THERE IS TO KNOW

www.dk.com

CONTENTS

4

Introduction

8

Essentials

20

Getting Around

42

Eating Out

62

Places to Stay

80

Shopping

110

Sightseeing

120

Sports and Leisure

136

Health

148

Emergencies

158

Menu Guide

167 / **195**
English–Italian
Dictionary
Italian–English
Dictionary

224
Numbers

INTRODUCTION

This book provides all the key words and phrases you are likely to need in everyday situations. It is grouped into themes, and key phrases are broken down into short sections, to help you build a wide variety of sentences. A lot of the vocabulary is illustrated to make it easy to remember, and "You may hear" boxes feature questions you are likely to hear. At the back of the book there is a menu guide, listing about 500 food terms, and a 2,000-word two-way dictionary. Numbers are listed on the last page of the book for quick reference.

NOUNS

All Italian nouns (words for things, people, and ideas) are masculine or feminine. The gender of singular nouns is usually shown by the word for "the": **il** or **lo** (masculine) and **la** (feminine). They change to **l'** before vowels. The plural forms are **i** or **gli** (masculine) and **le** (feminine).

ADJECTIVES

Most Italian adjectives change endings according to whether they describe a masculine or feminine, singular or plural word. In this book the singular masculine form is shown, followed by the alternative feminine ending:

I'm lost   **Mi sono perso/a**

"YOU"

There are two ways of saying "you" in Italian: **lei** (polite) and **tu** (familiar). In this book we have used **lei** throughout, as that is what you normally use with people you don't know.

VERBS

Verbs change according to whether they are in the singular or plural. In phrases where this happens, the singular form of the verb is followed by the plural form:

Where is/are...?   **Dov'è/Dove sono...?**

PRONUNCIATION GUIDE

Below each Italian word or phrase in this book, you will find a pronunciation guide in italics. Read it as if it were English and you should be understood, but remember that it is only a guide and for the best results you should listen to the native speakers in the audio app and try to mimic them. Some Italian sounds are different from those in English, so take note of how the letters below are pronounced.

a	like "a" in "car"
ai	like "i" in "mile"
ao, au	like "ow" in "cow"
c	before "a", "o", and "u", like "k" in "kite" before "i" and "e", like "ch" in "church"
cc	like "ch" in "church"
ch	like "k" in "keep"
e	like "e" in "pet"
ei	like "ay" in "day"
g	before "a", "o", and "u", like "g" in "get" before "i" and "e", like "j" in "jam"
gh	like "g" in "got"
gli	like "lli" in "million"
gn	like "ni" in "onion"
h	silent
i	like "ee" in "keep"
o	like "o" in "pot"
oi	like "oy" in "boy"
qu	like "qu" in "quick"
r	rolled
s	like "s" in "see" or "z" in "zoo"

sc	before "a", "o", and "u", like "sk" in "skip"
	before "i" or "e", like "sh" in "ship"
u	like "oo" in "boot"
z	like "ts" in "pets", or "ds" in "loads"

FREE EYEWITNESS TRAVEL PHRASE BOOK AUDIO APP

The audio app that accompanies this phrase book contains nearly 1,000 essential Italian words and phrases, spoken by native speakers, for use when travelling or when preparing for your trip.

HOW TO USE THE AUDIO APP

- Download the free app on your smartphone or tablet from the App Store or Google Play.
- Open the app and scan or key in the barcode on the back of your Eyewitness Phrase Book to add the book to your Library.
- Download the audio files for your language.
- The 🎧 symbol in the book indicates that there is audio for that section. Enter the page number from the book into the search field in the app to bring up the list of words and phrases for that page or section. You can then scroll up and down through the list to find the word or phrase you want.
- Tap a word or phrase to hear it.
- Swipe left or right to view the previous or next page.
- Add phrases you will use often to your Favourites.

ESSENTIALS

In this section, you will find the essential words and useful phrases you need for basic everyday talk and situations. Be aware of cultural differences when you're addressing Italian people, and also remember that they tend to be quite formal when they are greeting each other, using *signore* (for men), *signora* (for women) and *signorina* (for girls and younger women). These titles are also used with surnames.

GREETINGS

Hello	Salve *salveh*
Good evening	Buonasera *bwonaserah*
Good night	Buonanotte *bwonanotteh*
Goodbye	Arrivederci *arreevederchee*
Hi/bye!	Ciao/ciao! *chow*
Pleased to meet you	Piacere *pyachereh*
How are you?	Come sta? *komeh stah*
Fine, thanks	Bene, grazie *beneh gratsye*
You're welcome	Prego *pregoh*
My name is...	Mi chiamo... *mee kyamoh*
What's your name?	Come si chiama? *komeh see kyamah*
What's his/her name?	Lui/lei come si chiama? *looee/lay komeh see kyamah*
This is...	Questo/a è... *kwestoh/ah eh*
Nice to meet you	Lieto/a di conoscerla *lyetoh/ah dee konosherlah*
See you tomorrow	A domani *ah domanee*
See you soon	A presto *ah prestoh*

SMALL TALK

Yes/no	Sì/no *see/noh*
Please	Per favore *pehr favoreh*
Thank you (very much)	(Molte) grazie *(molteh) gratsye*
You're welcome	Prego *pregoh*
OK/fine	OK/bene *okay/beneh*
Pardon?	Scusi? *skoozee*
Excuse me	Mi scusi *mee skoozee*
Sorry	Mi dispiace *mee deespyacheh*
I don't know	Non so *non soh*
I don't understand	Non capisco *non kapeeskoh*
Could you repeat that?	Può ripetere? *pwo reepetereh*
I don't speak Italian	Non parlo italiano *non parloh eetalyanoh*
Do you speak English?	Parla inglese? *parlah eenglezeh*
What is the Italian for...?	Come si dice in italiano...? *komeh see deeche een eetalyanoh*
What's that called?	Come si chiama? *komeh see kyamah*
Can you tell me...	Mi può dire... *mee pwoh deereh*

TALKING ABOUT YOURSELF

I'm from...	Vengo da... *vengoh dah*
I'm...	Sono... *sonoh*
...American	...americano/a *amereekanoh/ah*
...English	...inglese *eengleseh*
...Canadian	...canadese *kanadezeh*
...Australian	...australiano/a *owstralyanoh/ah*
...single	...celibe/nubile *cheleebeh/noobeeleh*
...married	...sposato/a *sposatoh/ah*
...divorced	...divorziato/a *deevortsyatoh/ah*
I am...years old	Ho...anni *oh...annee*
I have...	Ho... *oh*
...a boyfriend	...un fidanzato *oon feedantsatoh*
...a girlfriend	...una fidanzata *oonah feedantsatah*
Where are you from?	Da dove viene? *dah doveh vyeneh*
Are you married?	È sposato/a? *eh sposatoh/ah*
Do you have children?	Ha figli? *ah feelye*

ESSENTIALS

SOCIALIZING

Do you live here?	Vive qui? *veeveh kwee*
Where do you live?	Dove vive? *doveh veeveh*
I am here...	Sono qui... *sonoh kwee*
...on holiday	...in vacanza *een vakantsah*
...on business	...per lavoro *pehr lavoroh*
I'm a student	Sono uno/a studente/studentessa *sonoh oonoh/ah stoodente/stoodentessah*
I work in...	Lavoro a... *lavoroh ah*
I am retired	Sono pensionato/a *sonoh pensyonatoh/ah*
Can I have...	Posso avere... *possoh avereh*
...your telephone number?	...il suo numero di telefono? *eel soowoh noomeroh dee telefonoh*
...your email address?	...il suo indirizzo e-mail? *eel soowoh eendeereedzo emayl*
It doesn't matter	Non importa *non eemportah*
Cheers	Cin cin *cheen cheen*
Do you mind if I smoke?	Le dispiace se fumo? *leh deespyache seh foomoh*
I don't drink/smoke	Non bevo/fumo *non bevoh/foomoh*
Are you alright?	Sta bene? *stah beneh*

LIKES AND DISLIKES

I like/love...
Mi piace/adoro...
mee pyacheh/adoroh

I don't like...
Non mi piace...
non mee pyacheh

I hate...
Detesto...
detestoh

I quite/really like...
Mi piace abbastanza/molto...
mee pyacheh abbastantsa/moltoh

Don't you like it?
Non le piace?
non leh pyacheh

I would like...
Vorrei...
vorray

My favourite is...
Il mio preferito è...
eel meeoh prefereetoh eh

I prefer...
Preferisco...
prefereeskoh

I think it's great
Penso che sia fantastico
pensoh keh sya fantasteeko

It's delicious
È delizioso/a
eh deleetsyozoh/ah

What would you like to do?
Cosa vorrebbe fare?
kozah vorrebbeh fareh

I don't mind
Non mi dispiace
non mee deespyacheh

Do you like...?
Le piace...?
leh pyacheh

YOU MAY HEAR...

Di cosa si occupa?
dee kozah see okoopah
What do you do?

È in vacanza?
eh een vakantsah
Are you on holiday?

DAYS OF THE WEEK

What day is it today?	Che giorno è oggi? *keh jornoh eh ojee*	**Friday**	venerdì *venerdee*
Sunday	domenica *domeneekah*	**Saturday**	sabato *sabatoh*
Monday	lunedì *loonedee*	**today**	oggi *odjee*
Tuesday	martedì *martedee*	**tomorrow**	domani *domanee*
Wednesday	mercoledì *merkoledee*	**yesterday**	ieri *yeree*
Thursday	giovedì *jovedee*	**in...days**	tra...giorni *trah...jornee*

THE SEASONS

primavera
preemaverah
spring

estate
estateh
summer

MONTHS

January	gennaio *jenayo*	**July**	luglio *loolyo*
February	febbraio *febrayo*	**August**	agosto *agostoh*
March	marzo *martso*	**September**	settembre *setembreh*
April	aprile *apreeleh*	**October**	ottobre *otobreh*
May	maggio *majjo*	**November**	novembre *novembreh*
June	giugno *joonyo*	**December**	dicembre *deechembreh*

autunno
owtoonnoh
autumn

inverno
eenvernoh
winter

TELLING THE TIME 🎧

What time is it?	Che ore sono? *keh oreh sonoh*
It's nine o'clock	Sono le nove *sonoh leh noveh*
...in the morning	...del mattino *del matteenoh*
...in the afternoon	...del pomeriggio *del pomereedjoh*
...in the evening	...della sera *dellah serah*

l'una
loonah
one o'clock

l'una e dieci
loonah eh deeaychee
ten past one

l'una e un quarto
loonah eh oon kwartoh
quarter past one

l'una e venti
loonah eh ventee
twenty past one

l'una e mezza
loonah eh medza
half past one

due meno un quarto
dooeh menoh oon kwartoh
quarter to two

due meno dieci
dooeh menoh deeaychee
ten to two

le due
leh dooeh
two o'clock

It's midday/midnight	È mezzogiorno/mezzanotte *eh medzojornoh/medzanotteh*
second	il secondo *eel sekondoh*
minute	il minuto *eel meenootoh*
hour	l'ora *lorah*
a quarter of an hour	un quarto d'ora *oon kwartoh dorah*
half an hour	mezz'ora *medzorah*
three-quarters of an hour	tre quarti d'ora *tray kwartee dorah*
late	tardi *tardee*
early/soon	presto/presto *prestoh*
What time does it start?	A che ora inizia? *ah keh orah eeneetsya*
What time does it finish?	A che ora finisce? *ah keh orah feeneesheh*
How long will it last?	Quanto tempo durerà? *kwantoh tempoh doorerah*

YOU MAY HEAR...

A presto	È in anticipo	È in ritardo
ah prestoh	*eh een anteecheepoh*	*eh een reetardoh*
See you later	**You're early**	**You're late**

THE WEATHER

What's the weather like?	Che tempo fa? *ke tempoh fah*
It's...	È... *eh*
...good	...buono *bwonoh*
...bad	...cattivo *kateevoh*
...warm	...mite *meeteh*
...hot	...caldo *kaldoh*
...cold	...freddo *freddoh*

È soleggiato
eh soledjatoh
It's sunny

È piovoso
eh pyovozoh
It's raining

È nuvoloso
eh noovolozoh
It's cloudy

È tempestoso
eh tempestozoh
It's stormy

What's the forecast?	Quali sono le previsioni? *kwalee sonoh leh preveezyonee*
What's the temperature?	Qual è la temperatura? *kwaleh lah temperatoorah*
It's...degrees	Ci sono...gradi *chee sonoh...gradee*
It's a beautiful day	È una bellissima giornata *eh oonah beleesseemah jornatah*
The weather's changing	Il tempo sta cambiando *eel tempoh stah kambyandoh*
Is it going to get colder/ hotter?	Farà più freddo/caldo? *farah pew freddoh/kaldoh*
It's cooling down	La temperatura sta scendendo *lah temperatoorah stah shendendoh*

Nevica
neveeka
It's snowing

È ghiacciato
eh gyatchyatoh
It's icy

C'è nebbia
che nebbyah
It's misty

È ventoso
eh ventozoh
It's windy

GETTING AROUND

Italy has an excellent road and motorway system
if you are travelling around the country by car,
although you have to pay a toll (*un pedaggio*) to
use the fast *autostrade* (motorways). Italian trains,
linking the main towns and cities, are fast, punctual
and surprisingly inexpensive. In large cities you can
get around by taxi, bus or tram. In Milan and Rome, there
is also the underground (*metropolitana*).

ASKING WHERE THINGS ARE

Excuse me	Mi scusi *mee skoozee*
Where is...	Dov'è... *doveh*
...the town centre?	...il centro della città? *eel chentroh dellah cheetah*
...the railway station?	...la stazione ferroviaria? *lah statsyoneh ferovyarya*
...a cash machine?	...uno sportello bancomat? *oonoh sportelloh bankomat*
How do I get to...?	Come posso arrivare a...? *komeh possoh arreevareh ah*
I'm going to...	Sto andando a... *stoh andandoh ah*
I'm looking for...	Sto cercando... *stoh cherkandoh*
I'm lost	Mi sono perso/a *mee sonoh persoh/ah*
Is it near?	Si trova qui vicino? *see trovah kwee veecheenoh*
Is there a...nearby?	C'è un...qui vicino? *che oon...kwee veecheenoh*
Is it far?	È lontano? *eh lontanoh*
How far is...	Quanto dista... *kwantoh deestah*
...the town hall?	...il municipio? *eel mooneecheepyo*
...the market?	...il mercato? *eel merkatoh*
Can I walk there?	Posso arrivarci a piedi? *possoh arreevarchee ah pyedee*

CAR AND BIKE RENTAL

Where is the car rental desk?	Dov'è l'ufficio dell'autonoleggio? *doveh loofeechyo del owtonoledjoh*
I want to hire...	Vorrei noleggiare... *vorray noledjareh*
...a car	...un'automobile *oon owtomobeeleh*
...a bicycle	...una bicicletta *oonah beecheeklettah*
for...days	per...giorni *pehr...jornee*
for a week	per una settimana *pehr oonah setteemanah*

la berlina
lah berleenah
saloon car

il portellone posteriore
eel portelloneh posteryoreh
hatchback

la motocicletta
lah motocheekletah
motorbike

lo scooter
loh scooter
scooter

la bicicletta da strada
lah beecheeklettah dah stradah
road bike

la mountain bike
lah mountain bike
mountain bike

for the weekend	per un fine settimana *pehr oon feeneh setteemanah*
I'd like...	Vorrei... *vorray*
...an automatic	...un'automobile con il cambio automatico *oon owtomobeeleh kon eel kambyo owtomateekoh*
...a manual	...un'automobile con il cambio manuale *oon owtomobeeleh kon eel kambyo manwaleh*
Here's my driving licence	Ecco la mia patente di guida *ekko lah mee-ah patenteh dee gweedah*
Can I hire a satnav?	Posso noleggiare... *possoh noledjareh*
Do you have a...	Avete... *aveteh*

il casco
eel kaskoh
cycling helmet

il lucchetto
eel lookettoh
lock

il seggiolino per bambini
eel sedjoleenoh pehr bambeenee
child seat

DRIVING

Is this the road to...?	È questa la strada per...? *eh kwestah lah stradah pehr*
Where is the nearest garage?	Qual è l'officina più vicina? *kwaleh lofeecheenah pew veecheenah*
I'd like...	Vorrei... *vorray*
...some petrol	...del carburante *del karbooranteh*
...40 litres of unleaded	...quaranta litri di benzina senza piombo *kwarantah leetree dee bentseenah sentsah pyomboh*
...30 litres of diesel	...trenta litri di gasolio *trentah leetree dee gazolyo*
Fill it up, please	Il pieno, per favore *eel pyenoh, pehr favoreh*
Where do I pay?	Dove pago? *doveh pagoh*
The pump number is...	La pompa numero... *lah pompah noomeroh...*
Can I pay by credit card?	Posso pagare con la carta di credito? *possoh pagareh kon lah kartah dee kredeetoh*
Can you check...	Può controllare... *pwo kontrollareh*
...the oil	...l'olio *lolyo*
...the tyre pressure	...la pressione dei pneumatici *lah pressyoneh day pneuhmateechee*

PARKING

Is there a car park nearby?	C'è un parcheggio nelle vicinanze? *che oon parkedjo nelleh veecheenantse*
Can I park here?	Posso parcheggiare qui? *possoh parkedjareh kwee*
Is it free?	È gratuito? *eh gratweetoh*
How much does it cost?	Quanto costa? *kwantoh kostah*
How much is it...	Quanto costa... *kwantoh kostah*
...per hour?	...all'ora? *alorah*
...per day?	...al giorno? *al jornoh*
...overnight?	...fino al giorno dopo? *feenoh al jornoh dopoh*

il portapacchi
eel portapakee
roofrack

il seggiolino
per bambini
*eel sedjoleenoh
pehr bambeenee*
child seat

stazione di servizio
h statsyoneh dee serveetsyo
*trol station

THE CAR

il bagagliaio
eel bagalyayo
boot

la marmitta
lah marmeetah
exhaust

la ruota
lah rwotah
wheel

lo sportello
loh sportelloh
door

INSIDE THE CAR

il poggiatesta
eel podjatestah
head rest

la maniglia
lah maneelya
handle

il sedile anteriore
eel sedeeleh anteryoreh
front seat

la
chiusura
*lah
kewsoorah*
door lock

la cintura
di sicurezza
*lah
cheentoorah
dee seekooredza*
seat belt

il sedile
posteriore
*eel sedeeleh
posteryoreh*
back seat

il parabrezza
eel parabredza
windscreen

il cofano
eel kofanoh
bonnet

i fari
ee faree
headlight

MEGANE

il pneumatico
eel pneoomateekoh
tyre

il motore
eel motoreh
engine

il paraurti
eel parowrtee
bumper

THE CONTROLS

l'impianto stereo
leempyantoh stereo
car stereo

le frecce lampeggianti
leh fretcheh lampedjantee
hazard lights

il tachimetro
eel takeemetroh
speedometer

l'airbag
lairbag
airbag

il cruscotto
eel krooskottoh
dashboard

il clacson
eel klakson
horn

la leva del
cambio
*lah levah
del kambyo*
gear stick

lo sterzo
loh stertso
steering wheel

ROAD SIGNS

senso unico
senzoh ooneeko
one way

rotatoria
rotatorya
roundabout

dare la precedenza
dareh lah prechedentsa
give way

divieto di sosta
deevyetoh dee sostah
no stopping

divieto di accesso
deevyetoh dee atchessoh
no entry

sosta vietata
sostah vyetatah
no parking

limite di velocità
leemeeteh dee velocheetah
speed limit

pericolo
pereekoloh
hazard

ON THE ROAD

il parchimetro
eel parkeemetroh
parking meter

il semaforo
eel semaforoh
traffic light

il vigile
eel veejeeleh
traffic policeman

l'attraversamento
pedonale
*latraversamentoh
pedonaleh*
pedestrian crossing

la cartina
lah karteenah
map

il parcheggio
per disabili
*eel parkedjoh pehr
deezabeelee*
disabled parking

l'autostrada
lowtostradah
motorway

la bretella
lah bretellah
sliproad

il telefono
d'emergenza
*eel telefonoh dee
emerjentsa*
emergency phone

T THE STATION

Where can I buy a ticket?	Dove posso acquistare un biglietto?
	doveh possoh akweestareh oon beelyettoh
Is there an automatic ticket machine?	C'è una biglietteria automatica?
	che oonah beelyettereeya owtomateekah
Two tickets to...	Due biglietti per...
	dooeh beelyettee pehr
I'd like...	Vorrei...
	vorray
...a single ticket to...	...un biglietto di sola andata per...
	oon beelyettoh dee solah andatah pehr
...a return ticket to...	...un biglietto di andata e ritorno per...
	oon beelyettoh dee andatah eh reetornoh pehr
...a first class ticket	...un biglietto di prima classe
	oon beelyettoh dee preemah klasseh
...a standard class ticket	...un biglietto di classe economica
	oon beelyettoh dee klasseh ekonomeekah
Is it a fast/slow train?	È un treno rapido/locale?
	eh oon trenoh rapeedoh/lokaleh

la biglietteria automatica
lah beelyetterya owtomateekah
automatic ticket machine

il biglietto
eel beelyettoh
ticket

I'd like to...	Vorrei... *vorray*
...reserve a seat	...prenotare un posto *prenotareh oon postoh*
...on the Eurostar to...	...sull'Eurostar per... *soolehoorostar pehr*
...book a couchette	...prenotare una cuccetta *prenotareh oonah koochettah*
Is there a reduction...	C'è una riduzione... *che oonah reedootsyoneh*
...for children?	...per i bambini? *pehr ee bambeenee*
...for students?	...per gli studenti? *pehr lyee stoodentee*
...for senior citizens?	...per gli anziani? *pehr lyee antsyanee*
Is there a restaurant car?	C'è una carrozza ristorante? *che oonah karrodza reestoranteh*
Do I stamp the ticket before boarding?	Devo vidimare il biglietto prima di salire in carrozza? *devoh veedeemareh eel beelyettoh preemah dee saleereh een karrodza*

YOU MAY HEAR...

Il treno parte dal binario...
eel trenoh parteh dal beenaryo
The train leaves from platform...

Deve cambiare treno
deveh kambyareh trenoh
You must change trains

TRAVELLING BY TRAIN

Do you have a timetable?
Ha un orario?
ah oon oraryo

What time is...
A che ora è...
ah ke orah eh

...the next train to...?
...il prossimo treno per...?
eel prosseemoh trenoh pehr

...the last train to...?
...l'ultimo treno per...?
loolteemoh trenoh pehr

Which platform does it leave from?
Da quale binario parte?
dah kwaleh beenaryo parteh

What time does it arrive in...?
A che ora arriva a...?
a ke orah arreevah ah

How long does it take?
Quanto tempo ci impiega?
kwantoh tempoh chee eempyegah

Is this the train for...?
È questo il treno per...?
eh kwestoh eel trenoh pehr

Is this the right platform for...?
È questo il binario giusto per...?
eh kwestoh eel beenaryo jewstoh pehr

Where is platform three?
Dov'è il binario tre?
doveh eel beenaryo treh

Does this train stop at...?
Questo treno ferma a...?
kwestoh trenoh fermah ah

YOU MAY HEAR...

Deve vidimare il biglietto
deveh veedeemareh eel beelyettoh
You must validate your ticket

Usi la macchinetta gialla
oozee lah makeenettah jallah
Use the yellow machine

Where do I change for...?	Dove devo cambiare per...? *doveh devoh kambyareh pehr*
Is this seat free?	È libero questo posto? *eh leeberoh kwestoh postoh*
I've reserved this seat	Ho prenotato questo posto *oh prenotatoh kwestoh postoh*
Do I get off here?	Devo scendere qui? *devoh shendereh kwee*
Where is the underground station?	Dov'è la stazione della metropolitana? *doveh lah statsyoneh dellah metropoleetanah*
Which line goes to...?	Quale linea arriva a...? *kwaleh leeneah arrivah ah*
How many stops is it?	Quante fermate sono? *kwanteh fermateh sonoh*

l'atrio
latryo
concourse

il treno
eel trenoh
train

la carrozza ristorante
lah karrodzah reestoranteh
dining car

la cuccetta
lah kootchettah
couchette

BUSES

When is the next bus to...?	Quando parte il prossimo autobus per...? *kwandoh parteh eel prosseemoh owtoboos pehr*
What is the fare to...?	Quanto costa un biglietto per...? *kwantoh kostah oon beelyettoh pehr*
Where is the bus stop?	Dov'è la fermata dell'autobus? *doveh lah fermatah del owtoboos*
Is this the bus stop for...?	È questa la fermata dell'autobus per...? *eh kwestah lah fermatah del owtoboos pehr*
Where can I buy a ticket?	Dove posso acquistare un biglietto? *doveh possoh akweestareh oon beelyettoh*
Can I pay on the bus?	Posso pagare sull'autobus? *possoh pagareh soolowtoboos*
Which buses go to the city centre?	Quali autobus raggiungono il centro? *kwalee owtoboos radjewngonoh eel chentroh*
Will you tell me when to get off?	Mi può dire quando devo scendere? *mee pwo deereh kwandoh devoh shendereh*

l'autobus
lowtoboos
bus

la stazione degli autobus
lah statsyoneh delyee owtoboos
bus station

TAXIS

Can I order a taxi?	Dove posso richiedere un taxi? *doveh possoh reekyedereh oon taxi*
I want a taxi to...	Desidero un taxi per... *deseederoh oon taxi pehr*
Can you take me to...?	Mi può portare a/in...? *mee pwo portareh ah/een*
Is it far?	È lontano? *eh lontanoh*
How much will it cost?	Quanto costa? *kwantoh kostah*
Can you drop me here?	Mi può far scendere qui? *mee pwo far shendereh kwee*
What do I owe you?	Quanto le devo? *kwantoh leh devoh*
I don't have any change	Non ho spiccioli *non oh speetchyolee*
Keep the change	Tenga il resto *tengah eel restoh*
Please can I have a receipt	Potrei avere la ricevuta, per favore *potray avereh lah reechevootah pehr favoreh*
Please wait for me	Mi aspetti, per favore *mee aspeteeh pehr favoreh*

il taxi
eel taxee
taxi

BOATS

Are there any boat trips?	Ci sono navi in partenza? *chee sonoh navee een partentsa*
Where does the boat leave from?	Dove parte la nave? *doveh parteh lah naveh*
When is...	Quando parte... *kwandoh parteh*
...the next boat to...?	...la prossima nave per...? *lah prosseemah naveh pehr*
...the first boat?	...la prima nave? *lah preemah naveh*
...the last boat?	...l'ultima nave? *loolteemah naveh*
I'd like two tickets for...	Vorrei due biglietti per... *vorray dooeh beelyettee pehr*
...the cruise	...la crociera *lah crotchyerah*

il traghetto
eel tragettoh
ferry

l'aliscafo
laleeskafoh
hydrofoil

la barca
a vela
*lah barka
ah velah*
yacht

l'hovercraft
lovercraft
hovercraft

...the river trip
...la gita sul fiume
lah jeetah sool fewmeh

How much is it for...
Quanto costa per...
kwantoh kostah pehr

...a car and two people?
...un'automobile e due persone?
oon owtomobeeleh eh dooeh personeh

...a family?
...una famiglia?
oona fameelyah

...a cabin?
...una cabina?
oonah kabeenah

Can I buy a ticket
on board?
Posso acquistare il biglietto
a bordo?
possoh akweestareh eel beelyettoh
ah bordoh

Is there wheelchair
access?
C'è un accesso per disabili?
che oon atchessoh pehr deezabeelee

ll motoscafo
eel motoscarfoh
motorboat

il salvagente
eel salvajenteh
lifebuoy

il catamarano
eel katamaranoh
catamaran

il giubbotto di
salvataggio
eel jewbottoh
dee salvatadjoh
life jacket

AIR TRAVEL

Which terminal do I need?	A quale terminal devo andare? *ah kwaleh terminahl devoh andareh*
Where do I check in?	Dove posso effettuare il check-in? *doveh possoh effettwareh eel check-in*
Where is...	Dove si trovano... *doveh see trovanoh*
...the arrivals hall?	...gli arrivi? *lyee arreevee*
...the departures hall?	...le partenze? *leh partentse*
...the boarding gate?	...le uscite d'imbarco? *leh oosheeteh deembarkoh*
I'm travelling...	Viaggio... *vyadjoh*
...economy	...in classe economica *een klasseh ekonomeeka*
...business class	... in business class *een business class*

la sacca da viaggio
lah sakah dah vyadjo
holdall

il passaporto
eel passaportoh
passport

il pasto a bordo
eel pastoh
ah bordoh
flight meal

la carta
d'imbarco
lah kartah
deembarko
boarding pass

I'm checking in one suitcase	Desidero imbarcare un bagaglio *deseederoh embarkareh oon bagalyo*
I packed it myself	Ho preparato io il bagaglio *oh preparatoh eeoh eel bagalyo*
I have one piece of hand luggage	Ho un unico bagaglio a mano *oh oon ooneeko bagalyo ah manoh*
How much is excess baggage?	A quanto ammonta il peso in eccesso? *ah kwantoh amontah eel pezoh een etchessoh*
Will a meal be served?	Sarà servito un pasto? *sarah serveetoh oon pastoh*
I'd like...	Vorrei... *vorray*
...a window seat	...un posto vicino al finestrino *oon postoh veecheenoh al feenestreenoh*
...an aisle seat	...un posto vicino al corridoio *oon postoh veecheenoh al koreedoyo*

YOU MAY HEAR...

Il suo passaporto/biglietto, per favore
eel soowo passaportoh/ beelyettoh pehr favoreh
Your passport/ticket, please

È sua questa borsa?
eh soowa kwestah borsah
Is this your bag?

AT THE AIRPORT

Here's my...	Ecco... *ekko*
...boarding pass	...la mia carta d'imbarco *la meeah karta deembarkoh*
...passport	...il mio passaporto *eel meeoh passaportoh*
Can I change some money?	Potrei cambiare del denaro? *potray kambyareh dehl denaroh?*
What is the exchange rate?	Qual è il tasso di cambio? *kwaleh eel tassoh dee kambyo*
Is the flight delayed?	Il volo è in ritardo? *eel voloh eh een reetardoh*

banco del check-in
banko del chek een
check-in

ufficio di cambio
oofeechyo dee kambyo
**currency exchange
booth**

il controllo passaporti
*eel kontrolloh
passaportee*
passport control

il negozio duty-free
eel negotsyo dootee free
duty-free shop

il ritiro bagagli
eel reeteeroh bagalyee
baggage reclaim

il pilota
eel peelotah
pilot

l'aeroplano
lahehroplahnoh
aeroplane

l'assistente di volo
lasseestenteh dee voloh
air stewardess

How late is it?
Quanto porta di ritardo?
kwantoh portah dee reetardoh

Which gate does flight...
leave from?
Qual è l'uscita del volo...?
kwaleh loosheetah del voloh

What time do I board?
A che ora ci imbarchiamo?
ah keh orah chee eembarkyamoh

When does the gate
close?
Quando chiude l'uscita d'imbarco?
*kwandoh kewdeh loosheetah
deembarkoh*

Where are the trolleys?
Dove sono i carrelli?
doveh sonoh ee karrelee

Here is the reclaim tag
Ecco la ricevuta dei bagagli
ekko lah reechevootah day bagalye

I can't find my baggage
Non trovo i miei bagagli
non trovoh ee myayee bagalye

EATING OUT

It is not difficult to eat well and inexpensively in Italy. You can choose from cafés and bars, which serve a variety of drinks, snacks and light meals, *osterie* and *trattorie* (small family-run restaurants which serve local and traditional dishes) and *pizzerie* (for pizzas and pasta). If you want a gastronomic meal in more formal surroundings, you can eat at more expensive *ristorante* but you may have to book in advance at the popular ones.

MAKING A RESERVATION

I'd like to book a table...	Vorrei prenotare un tavolo... *voray prenotareh oon tavoloh*
...for lunch/dinner	...per pranzo/cena *pehr prandzo/ chenah*
...for four people	...per quattro persone *pehr kwatroh personeh*
...for this evening	...per questa sera *pehr kwestah serah*
...for tomorrow at one	...per l'una di domani *pehr loonah dee domanee*
...for today	...per oggi *pehr odjee*
Do you have a table earlier/later?	Ha un tavolo prima/più tardi? *ah oon tavoloh preemah/pew tardee*
My name is...	Il cognome è... *eel konyomeh eh*
My telephone number is...	Il mio numero di telefono è... *eel meeoh noomeroh dee telefonoh eh*
Do you take credit cards?	Accettate carte di credito? *atchettateh karteh dee kredeetoh*
I have a reservation	Ho una prenotazione *oh oonah prenotatsyoneh*
in the name of...	a nome di... *ah nomeh dee*
We haven't booked	Non abbiamo prenotato *non abyamoh prenotatoh*
Can we sit here?	Possiamo sederci qui? *possyamoh sederchee kwee*
We'd like to eat outside	Vorremmo mangiare fuori *vorremoh manjareh fworee*

ORDERING A MEAL

Can we see the menu?	Possiamo vedere il menù? *possyamoh vedereh eel menoo*
...the wine list?	...la carta dei vini? *lah kartah day veenee*
Do you have...	Ha... *ah*
...a set menu?	...un menù fisso? *oon menoo feesoh*
...a fixed-price menu?	...un menù a prezzo fisso? *oon menoo ah predzo feesoh*
...a children's menu?	...un menù per bambini? *oon menoo pehr bambeenee*
...an à la carte menu	...un menù alla carta? *oon menoo allah kartah*
What are today's specials?	Qual è la specialità del giorno? *kwaleh lah spechyaleetah del jornoh*
What is this?	Cos'è questo/a? *kozeh kwestoh/ah*

YOU MAY HEAR...

Ha prenotato?
ah prenotatoh
Do you have a reservation?

Si sieda per favore
see syedah pehr favoreh
Please be seated

A nome di?
ah nomeh dee
In what name?

Vuole ordinare?
vwoleh ordeenareh
Are you ready to order?

Are there any vegetarian dishes?	Avete dei piatti vegetariani? *aveteh day pyatee vejetaryanee*
I can't eat...	Non posso mangiare... *non possoh manjareh*
...dairy foods	...i latticini *ee latteecheenee*
...nuts	...la frutta secca *lah frootah sekah*
...wheat	...il frumento *eel froomentoh*
To drink, I'll have...	Da bere, vorrei... *dah bereh vorray*
Can we have...	Possiamo avere... *possyamoh avereh*
...some water	...dell'acqua? *delakwa*
...some bread?	...del pane? *del paneh*
...the dessert menu?	...il menù dei dolci? *eel menoo day dolchee*

READING THE MENU...

gli antipasti *lyee anteepastee* **starters**	i secondi *ee sekondee* **main courses**	i formaggi *ee formadjee* **cheeses**
i primi *ee preemee* **first courses**	i contorni *ee kontornee* **vegetables**	i dolci *ee dolchee* **desserts**

COMPLAINING

I didn't order this	Non ho ordinato questo/a *non oh ordeenatoh kwestoh/ah*
When is our food coming?	Quando arriva il cibo? *kwandoh arreevah eel cheeboh*
We can't wait any longer	Non possiamo aspettare oltre *non possyamoh aspettareh oltreh*

PAYING

The bill, please	Il conto, per favore *eel kontoh pehr favoreh*
Can we pay separately?	Possiamo pagare separatamente? *possyamoh pagareh separatamenteh*
Can I have...	Posso avere... *possoh avereh*
...a receipt?	...la ricevuta? *lah reechevootah*
...an itemized bill?	...una ricevuta dettagliata? *oonah reechevootah detalyatah*
Is service included?	Il servizio è incluso? *eel serveetsyo eh eenkloozoh*

YOU MAY HEAR...

Non accettiamo carte di credito
non atchetyamoh karteh dee kredeetoh
We don't take credit cards

Digiti il PIN
deejeetee eel peen
Please enter your PIN

CROCKERY AND CUTLERY

il piattino
eel pyateenoh
side plate

la scodella
lah skodellah
bowl

il sale
eel saleh
salt

il pepe
eel pepeh
pepper

il cucchiaio
eel kookyayo
dessert spoon

il cucchiaino
eel kookyaeenoh
teaspoon

la tazza e il piattino
lah tadza eh eel pyateenoh
cup and saucer

il bicchiere
eel beekyereh
glass

il tovagliolo
eel tovalyoloh
napkin

la forchetta
lah forkettah
fork

il coltello
eel koltelloh
knife

il piatto piano
eel pyato pyanoh
dinner plate

AT THE CAFÉ OR BAR

The menu, please	Il menù, per favore *eel menooh pehr favoreh*
Do you have...?	Ha...? *ah*
What fruit juices/herb teas do you have?	Quali succhi di frutta/tisane ha? *kwalee sookee dee frootah/teezaneh ah*
I'd like...	Vorrei... *juh vorray*

un caffellatte
oon kaffelatteh
white coffee

un caffè
oon kaffeh
black coffee

un espresso
oon espressoh
espresso

un cappuccino
oon kapootcheenoh
cappuccino

YOU MAY HEAR...

Cosa desidera?
kozah deseederah
What would you like?

Altro?
altroh
Anything else?

Prego
pregoh
You're welcome

un tè al latte
oon teh al latteh
tea with milk

un tè al limone
oon teh al leemoneh
tea with lemon

un tè alla menta
oon teh allah mentah
mint tea

un tè verde
oon teh verdeh
green tea

una camomilla
oonah kamomeelah
camomile tea

una cioccolata calda
oonah chokolatah kaldah
hot chocolate

A bottle of...	Una bottiglia di... *oonah botteelya dee*
A glass of...	Un bicchiere di... *oon beekyereh dee*
A cup of...	Una tazza di... *oonah tadza dee*
With lemon/milk	Con limone/latte *kon leemoneh/latteh*
Another...please	Un altro/a...per favore *oon altroh/ah…pehr favoreh*
The same again, please	Me ne porta ancora, per favore *meh neh portah ankorah pehr favoreh*

CAFÉ AND BAR DRINKS

un succo di ananas
oon sookoh dee ananas
pineapple juice

un succo di mela
oon sookoh dee melah
apple juice

una spremuta d'arancia
oonah spremootah daranchya
fresh orange juice

una limonata
oonah leemonatah
lemonade

un succo d'uva
oon sookoh doovah
grape juice

un succo di pomodoro
oon sookoh dee pomodoroh
tomato juice

un crodino
oon krodeenoh
Crodino

una coca cola
oonah kokakolah
cola

un caffè shakerato
oon kaffeh shakeratoh
iced coffee

un campari
oon kamparee
Campari

una grappa
oonah grappah
Grappa

una birra
oonah beerrah
beer

acqua minerale
akwa meeneraleh
mineral water

un prosecco
oon prosekoh
sparkling wine

un vino bianco
oon veenoh byankoh
white wine

un vino rosso
oon veenoh rossoh
red wine

YOU MAY HEAR...

In bottiglia o alla spina?
een botteelya oh allah speenah
Bottled or draught?

Liscia o gassata?
leesha oh gassatah
Still or sparkling?

Con ghiaccio?
kon gyachyo
With ice?

BAR SNACKS

un tramezzino
oon tramedzeenoh
sandwich

un panino
oon paneenoh
panino

le olive
leh oliveh
olives

le noccioline
leh notcholeeneh
nuts

il condimento
eel kondimentoh
dressing

l'insalata
leensalatah
salad

i biscotti
ee beeskottee
biscuits

la bruschetta
lah brooskettah
bruschetta

il gelato
eel jelatoh
ice cream

i maritozzi
ee mareetodzee
cream buns

FAST FOOD

Can I have...

Posso avere...
possoh avereh

...to eat in/take away

...da mangiare qui/da portare via
dah manjareh kwee/dah portareh vee-ah

un hamburger
oon amboorger
hamburger

un hamburger
di pollo
*oon amboorger
dee polloh*
chicken burger

una piadina
arrotolata
*oonah pyadeenah
arotolatah*
wrap

un hot dog
oon otdog
hot dog

un kebab
oon kebab
kebab

le patatine
leh patateeneh
French fries

il pollo fritto
eel polloh freetoh
fried chicken

la pizza
lah peedza
pizza

BREAKFAST

Can I have...	Posso avere... *possoh avereh*
...some milk	...del latte? *del latteh*
...some sugar	dello zucchero? *delloh tsookeroh*
...some artificial sweetener	...del dolcificante? *del dolcheefeekanteh*
...some butter	...del burro? *del booroh*
...some jam?	...della marmellata? *dellah marmellatah*
...some salt/pepper?	...del sale/del pepe? *del saleh/del pehpeh*

un caffè
oon kaffeh
coffee

un tè
oon teh
tea

una cioccolata
calda
oonah
chokolatah
kaldah
hot chocolate

una spremuta
d'arancia
oonah
spremootah
daranchya
orange juice

un succo di mela
oon sookoh dee
melah
apple juice

il pane
eel paneh
bread

un panino
oon paneenoh
bread roll

il miele
eel myeleh
honey

un cornetto
oon kornettoh
croissant

la marmellata
lah marmellatah
marmalade

un cornetto al
cioccolato
*oon kornettoh
al chokolatoh*
**chocolate
croissant**

le uova
strapazzate
*leh wovah
strapadzateh*
**scrambled
eggs**

l'uovo sodo
lwovoh sodoh
boiled egg

l'uovo in camicia
*lwovoh een
kameecha*
poached egg

lo yoghurt
alla frutta
*loh yogoort
allah frootah*
fruit yoghurt

la frutta fresca
*lah frootah
freskah*
fresh fruit

FIRST COURSES

la minestra
lah meenestrah
soup

il brodo
eel brodoh
broth

la zuppa di
pesce
*lah tsoopah dee
pesheh*
fish soup

il minestrone
*eel
meenestroneh*
minestrone

il prosciutto
crudo
*eel proshewtoh
kroodoh*
cured ham

i gamberi alla
griglia
*ee gamberee
allah greelya*
grilled prawns

la bresaola
lah bresaolah
bresaola

il risotto
eel reezottoh
risotto

gli gnocchi
lyee nyokee
gnocchi

i tortelloni
ee tortellonee
tortelloni

le sarde al saor
leh sardeh al saor
**Venetian-style
sardines**

gli spaghetti
alla bolognese
*lyee spagetee
alla bolonyeseh*
**spaghetti
bolognese**

gli spaghetti
alla vongole
*lyee spagetee
alla vongoleh*
**spaghetti
with clams**

gli spaghetti
alla carbonara
*lyee spagetee
alla karbonara*
**spaghetti
carbonara**

l'antipasto misto
*lanteepastoh
meestoh*
mixed antipasto

i cannelloni
ee kannellonee
cannelloni

la frittata
lah freetatah
omelette

l'antipasto freddo
*lanteepastoh
freddoh*
**antipasto of
cold meats**

la bagna cauda
*lah banya
cowdah*
**hot anchovy
dip**

l'antipasto
di mare
*lanteepastoh
dee mareh*
**seafood
antipasto**

MAIN COURSES

I would like...	Vorrei... *vorray*	...the liver	...il fegato *eel fegatoh*
...the chicken	...il pollo *eel polloh*	roast	arrosto *arrostoh*
...the duck	...l'anatra *lanatrah*	baked	al forno *al fornoh*
...the lamb	...l'agnello *lanyelloh*	grilled	alla griglia *allah greelya*
...the pork	...il maiale *eel mayaleh*	on skewers	allo spiedo *alloh spyedoh*
...the beef	...il manzo *eel mandzo*	barbecued	al barbecue *al barbekew*
...the steak	...la bistecca *lah beestekkah*	poached	in camicia *een kameechya*
...the veal	...il vitello *eel veeteloh*	boiled	lesso/sodo *lessoh/sodoh*

YOU MAY SEE...

i frutti di mare
ee frootee dee mareh
seafood

il pesce
eel pesheh
fish

YOU MAY HEAR...

Come desidera la bistecca?
komeh deseederah lah beestekkah
How do you like your steak?

Al sangue, a cottura media o ben cotta?
al sangweh, ah kottoorah medya oh ben kottah
Rare, medium rare or well done?

fried	fritto *freetoh*	**stewed**	stufato *stoofatoh*
pan-fried/ sautéed	in padella/saltato *een padellah/saltatoh*	**...with Parmesan cheese**	...con il parmigiano *kon eel parmeejanoh*
stuffed	farcito *farcheetoh*		

il pollame
eel pollameh
poultry

la carne
lah karneh
meat

SALADS AND SIDE DISHES

l'insalata
verde
*leensalatah
verdeh*
green salad

l'insalata mista
*leensalatah
meestah*
mixed salad

il radicchio
alla griglia
*eel radeekkyo
allah greelya*
grilled radicchio

gli asparagi
lyee asparajee
asparagus

gli spinaci
*lyee
speenachee*
spinach

le verdure
al vapore
*leh verdooreh
al vaporeh*
**steamed
vegetables**

le patatine
fritte
*leh patateeneh
freeteh*
chips

la pasta
lah pastah
pasta

la polenta
lah polentah
polenta

il riso
eel reezoh
rice

DESSERTS

lo zabaglione
loh tsabalyoneh
zabaglione

il gelato
eel jelatoh
ice cream

la mousse di
cioccolato
*lah moos dee
chokolatoh*
**chocolate
mousse**

la crostata
di frutta
*lah krostatah
dee frootah*
fruit tart

la cassata
lah kassatah
cassata

il tiramisù
eel teerameesoo
tiramisù

il sorbetto
eel sorbettoh
sorbet

la torta
lah tortah
cake

la crostata di
ricotta
*lah krostatah
dee reekottah*
ricotta tart

la crostata di
nocciole
*lah krostatah
dee nochyoleh*
hazelnut tart

PLACES TO STAY

Italy has a wide range of places to stay, depending
on your personal preference and budget. These range
from elegant hotels in former *palazzi* to smaller *alberghi*,
locande (one-star hotels) and family-run *pensioni*. If you
want a self-catering option, however, you can choose
to rent a seaside apartment or a country villa, or find
a campsite to park your caravan or put up your tent.

MAKING A RESERVATION

I'd like...	Vorrei... *vorray*
...to make a reservation	...fare una prenotazione *fareh oonah prenotatsyoneh*
...a double room	...una camera doppia *oonah kamerah doppya*
...a twin-bedded room	...una camera a due letti *oonah kamerah ah dooeh lettee*
...a single room	...una camera singola *oonah kamerah seengolah*
...a family room	...una camera familiare *oonah kamerah fameelyareh*
...a disabled person's room	...una camera per disabili *oonah kamerah pehr deezabeelee*
...with a bath/shower	...con bagno/doccia *kon banyo/dotchya*
...with a sea view	...con vista sul mare *kon veestah sool mareh*
...with a balcony	...con balcone *kon balkoneh*
...for two nights	...per due notti *pehr dooeh nottee*
...for a week	...per una settimana *pehr oonah setteemanah*
Is breakfast included?	La colazione è inclusa? *lah kolatsyoneh eh eenkloosah*
How much is it...	Quanto costa... *kwantoh kostah*
...per night?	...a notte? *ah notteh*
...per week?	...alla settimana? *allah setteemanah*

CHECKING IN

I have a reservation in the name of...	Ho una prenotazione a nome di... *oh oonah prenotatsyoneh ah nomeh dee*
Do you have...	Ha... *ah*
I'd like...	Vorrei... *vorray*
...the keys for room...	...le chiavi della camera... *leh kyavee dellah kamerah*
...a wake-up call at...	...la sveglia alle... *lah svelya alleh*
What time is...	A che ora servite... *ah ke orah serveeteh*
...breakfast?	...la colazione? *lah kolatsyoneh*
...dinner?	...la cena? *lah chenah*

un facchino
oon fakeenoh
porter

il mini bar
eel meenee bar
mini bar

il servizio in
camera
*eel serveetsyo
een kamerah*
room service

gli ascensori
lyee ashensoree
lifts

IN YOUR ROOM

Do you have...	Ha... *ah*
another...	un altro/a... *oon altroh/ah*
some more...	altri/e... *altree/eh*
I've lost my key	Ho perso la mia chiave *oh persoh lah meeah kiaveh*

le coperte
leh koperteh
blankets

i cuscini
ee koosheenee
pillows

un adattatore
oon adatatoreh
adapter

una lampadina
oonah lampadeenah
light bulb

YOU MAY HEAR...

Il suo numero di camera è...
eel soo-oh noomeroh dee kamerah eh
Your room number is...

Ecco la sua chiave
ekko lah sooah kiaveh
Here is your key

IN THE HOTEL

The room is...	La camera è... *lah kamerah e*
...too hot	...troppo calda *troppoh kaldah*
...too cold	...troppo fredda *troppoh freddah*
...too small	...troppo piccola *troppoh peekolah*
The window won't open	La finestra non si apre *lah feenestrah non see apreh*
The TV doesn't work	Il televisore non funziona *eel televeezoreh non funtsyonah*

il bollitore
eel bolleetoreh
kettle

il radiatore
eel radyatoreh
radiator

il termostato
eel termostatoh
thermostat

la camera singola
lah kamerah seengolah
single room

la camera doppia
lah kamerah doppya
double room

il numero della camera
eel noomeroh dellah kamerah
room number

il televisore
eel televeezoreh
television

il telecomando
eel telekomandoh
remote control

l'appendiabiti
lappendeeabeetee
coat hanger

la veneziana
lah venetsyanah
Venetian blind

CHECKING OUT

When do I have to vacate the room?
Quando devo lasciare la stanza?
kwandoh devoh lasheeareh lah standza

Is there a porter to carry my bags?
C'è un facchino per portare le mie valigie?
che oon fakkeenoh pehr portareh leh meeye valeejeh

Can I have the bill, please?
Posso avere il conto?
possoh avereh eel kontoh

Can I pay...
Posso pagare...
possoh pagareh

...by credit card?
...con la carta di credito?
kon lah kartah dee kredeetoh

...cash?
...in contanti?
een kontantee

I'd like a receipt
Vorrei la ricevuta
vorray lah reechevootah

IN THE BATHROOM

gli asciugamani
lyee ashewgamanee
towels

l'accappatoio
lakappatoyo
bathrobe

il sapone
eel saponeh
soap

il deodorante
eel dehodoranteh
deodorant

il dentifricio
eel denteefreechyo
toothpaste

il bagnoschiuma
eel banyoskewmah
bubble bath

il bidet
eel beedeh
bidet

il docciaschiuma
eel dotchyaskwemah
shower gel

la vasca
da bagno
lah vaska
dah banyo
bathtub

la crema
per il corpo
lah kremah
pehr eel korpoh
body lotion

lo spazzolino da denti
*loh spatsoleenoh
dah dentee*
toothbrush

l'asciugacapelli
lashewgakapellee
hairdryer

il rasoio elettrico
eel rasoyo eletreeko
electric razor

la schiuma
da barba
*lah skewmah
dah barbah*
shaving foam

il rasoio
eel rasoyo
razor

il colluttorio
eel kolootoryo
mouthwash

lo shampoo
loh shampoh
shampoo

il balsamo
eel balsamoh
conditioner

il tagliaunghie
eel talyaoongye
nail clippers

le forbici
per unghie
*leh forbeechee
pehr oongye*
nail scissors

SELF-CATERING

Can we have...	Possiamo avere...
	possyamoh avereh
...the key, please?	...la chiave, per favore?
	lah kiaveh pehr favoreh
...an extra bed?	...un letto extra?
	oon lettoh extrah
...a child's bed?	...un lettino?
	oon letteenoh
...more cutlery/ crockery	...più posate/stoviglie
	pew posateh/stoveelye
Where is...	Dov'è...
	doveh
...the fusebox?	...la scatola dei fusibili?
	lah skatolah day fooseebeelee
...the stopcock?	...il rubinetto d'arresto?
	eel roobeenettoh darrestoh

il termoconvettore
eel termokonverteetoreh
convector heater

il ventilatore
eel venteelatoreh
fan

il lettino
eel leteenoh
cot

il seggiolone
eel sedjoloneh
high chair

...the nearest shop?	...il negozio più vicino? *eel negotsyo pew veecheenoh*
Do you do babysitting?	Offrite un servizio di babysitting? *offreeteh oon serveetsyo dee babyseetteeng*
How does the heating work?	Come funziona il riscaldamento? *komeh foontsyonah eel reeskaldamentoh*
Is there...	C'è... *che*
...air conditioning?	...l'aria condizionata? *larya kondeetsyonatah*
...central heating?	...il riscaldamento centralizzato? *eel reeskaldamentoh chentraleedzatoh*
When does the cleaner come?	Quando passa l'addetto alle pulizie? *kwandoh passah ladettoh alleh pooleetsye*
Where do I put the rubbish?	Dove posso buttare l'immondizia? *doveh possoh bootareh leemondeetsyah*
Do you take pets?	Accettate animali domestici? *atchettateh aneemalee domesteechee*

il cane
eel kaneh
dog

IN THE VILLA

Is there an inventory?	C'è un inventario? *che oon eenventaryo*
Where is this item?	Dove si trova questo articolo? *doveh see trovah kwestoh arteekoloh*
I need...	Ho bisogno di... *oh beezonyo dee*
...an extension lead	...una prolunga *oonah proloongah*
...a torch	...una torcia *oonah torchya*
...matches	...dei fiammiferi *day fyameeferee*

il forno a microonde
eel fornoh ah meekrohondeh
microwave

il ferro da stiro
eel ferroh dah steeroh
iron

l'asse da stiro
lasseh dah steeroh
ironing board

il mocio e il secchio
eel mochyo eh eel sekkyo
mop and bucket

la paletta e la scopetta
lah palettah eh lah skopettah
dustpan and bush

il detersivo
eel deterseevoh
detergent

PROBLEM SOLVING

The shower doesn't work — La doccia non funziona / *lah dotchya non foontsyonah*

The toilet is leaking — Il water perde acqua / *eel vater perdeh akwa*

Can you mend it today? — Può aggiustarlo oggi? / *pwo adjewstarloh odjee*

There's no... — Non c'è... / *non che*

...electricity/gas — ...elettricità/gas / *eletreecheetah/gas*

...water — ...acqua / *akwa*

la lavatrice / *lah lavatreeche* / **washing machine**

il frigorifero / *eel freegoreeferoh* / **fridge**

l'estintore / *lesteentoreh* / **fire extinguisher**

il lucchetto e la chiave / *eel lookettoh eh lah kiaveh* / **lock and key**

il rivelatore di fumo / *eel reevelatoreh dee foomoh* / **smoke alarm**

la pattumiera / *lah patoomyerah* / **rubbish bin**

KITCHEN EQUIPMENT

il tagliere
eel talyehreh
chopping board

la teglia da forno
lah telya dah fornoh
baking tray

la frusta
lah froostah
whisk

il coltello da cucina
eel koltelloh dah koocheenah
kitchen knife

lo sbucciatore
loh sbootchyatoreh
peeler

l'apriscatole
lapreeskatoleh
can opener

l'apribottiglie
lapreeboteelyeh
bottle opener

il cavatappi
eel kavatappee
corkscrew

la grattuggia
lah grattoojah
grater

il cucchiaio di legno
eel kookyayo dee lenyo
wooden spoon

la padella
lah padellah
frying pan

il colapasta
eel kolapastah
colander

la spatola
lah spatolah
spatula

la pentola
la pentolah
saucepan

la griglia
lah greelya
grill pan

la casseruola
lah kasserwolah
casserole dish

l'insalatiera
leensalatyerah
mixing bowl

il grembiule
eel grembewleh
apron

i guanti da forno
ee gwantee dah fornoh
oven gloves

il frullatore
eel froolatoreh
blender

CAMPING

Where is the nearest...	Dov'è il più vicino... *doveh eel pew veecheenoh*
...campsite?	...campeggio? *kampedjoh*
...caravan site?	...campeggio per camper? *kampedjoh pehr kamper*
Can we camp here?	Possiamo accamparci qui? *possyamoh akamparchee kwee*
Do you have any vacancies?	C'è posto disponibile? *che postoh deesponeebeeleh*
What is the charge...	Quanto costa... *kwantoh kostah*
...per night?	...per notte? *pehr notteh*
...per week?	...per settimana? *pehr setteemanah*
Does the price include...	Il costo include... *eel kostoh eenkloodeh*
...electricity?	...l'elettricità? *leletreecheetah*
...hot water?	...l'acqua calda? *lakwa kaldah*
We want to stay for...	Desideriamo rimanere per... *deseederyamoh reemanereh pehr*

la tenda
lah tendah
tent

la corda
lah kordah
guy rope

il picchetto
eel peekkettoh
tent peg

Can I rent...	Posso noleggiare... *possoh noledjareh*
...a tent?	...una tenda? *oonah tendah*
...a barbecue?	...un barbecue? *oon barbecue*
Where are...	Dove sono... *doveh sonoh*
...the toilets?	...i servizi? *ee serveetsee*
...the dustbins?	...i bidoni dell'immondizia? *ee beedonee del eemondeetsya*
Are there...	Ci sono... *chee sonoh*
...showers?	...docce? *dotcheh*
...laundry facilities?	...servizi di lavanderia? *serveetsee dee lavanderya*
Is there...	C'è... *che*
...a swimming pool?	...una piscina? *oonah peesheenah*
...a shop?	...un negozio? *oon negotsyo*

YOU MAY HEAR...

Non accendere il
fuoco
*non atchendereh
eel fwoko*
Don't light a fire

Non bere l'acqua
non bereh lakwa
**Don't drink
the water**

AT THE CAMPSITE

il bollitore
eel boleetoreh
camping kettle

il thermos
eel termos
vacuum flask

il barbecue
eel barbecue
barbecue

il fornello da campeggio
eel fornelloh dah kampedjoh
camping stove

l'acqua in bottiglia
lakwa een botteelya
bottled water

il frigo portatile
eel freegoh portateeleh
coolbox

il sacco a pelo
eel sakko ah peloh
sleeping bag

il materasso gonfiabile
eel materassoh gonfyabeeleh
air mattress

la torcia
lah torchya
torch

lo zaino
loh dzaeenoh
backpack

il secchio
eel sekyo
bucket

il maglio
eel malyo
mallet

il cestino da picnic
*eel chesteenoh
dah picnic*
picnic hamper

il filtro solare
eel feeltroh solareh
sunscreen

i cerotti
ee cherotee
plaster

la matassa
di spago
*lah matassah
dee spagoh*
ball of string

gli scarponi
da montagna
*lye skarponee
dah montanya*
walking boots

la bussola
lah boosolah
compass

SHOPPING

As well as shopping malls, supermarkets and specialist shops, Italy has many picturesque open-air markets in town squares and on high streets where you can buy food, clothes and even antiques relatively cheaply. Most shops are open between 8.30am and 12.30pm, and 3.30pm to 7.30pm from Tuesday to Saturday. Be aware that many stores and food shops are shut on Monday mornings or all day Mondays.

IN THE STORE

I'm looking for...

Sto cercando...
stoh cherkandoh

Do you have...?

Avete...?
aveteh

I'm just looking

Sto solo guardando
stoh soloh gwardandoh

I'm being served

Mi stanno già servendo
mee stannoh jah servendoh

Do you have any more of these?

Ne avete ancora?
eh aveteh ankorah

How much is this?

Quanto costa questo?
wantoh kostah kwestoh

Have you anything cheaper?

Avete qualcosa di
meno costoso?
*aveteh kwalkosah dee
menoh kostosoh*

I'll take this one

Prendo questo/a
prendoh kwestoh/ah

Where can I pay?

Dove posso pagare?
doveh possoh pagareh

I'll pay...

Desidero pagare...
deseederoh pagareh

...in cash

...in contanti
een kontantee

...by credit card

...con la carta di credito
kon lah kartah dee kredeetoh

Can I have a receipt?

Mi può fare lo scontrino?
mee pwo fareh loh skontreenoh

I'd like to exchange this

Vorrei cambiare questo/a
vorray kambyareh kwestoh/ah

IN THE BANK

I'd like...	Desidero... *deseederoh*
...to make a withdrawal	...effettuare un prelievo *effettwareh oon prelyevoh*
...to pay in some money	...effettuare un deposito *effettwareh oon deposeetoh*
...to change some money	...cambiare del denaro *kambyareh del denaroh*
...into euros	...in euro *een ehooroh*
...into dollars/sterling	...in dollari/sterline *een dohlaree/sterleeneh*
Here is my passport	Ecco il mio passaporto *ekko eel meeo passaportoh*
My name is...	Mi chiamo... *mee kiamoh*
My account number is...	Il mio numero di conto è... *eel meeo noomeroh dee kontoh eh*
My bank details are...	I miei dettagli bancari sono... *ee myayee dettalyee bankaree sonoh*

il passaporto
eel passaportoh
passport

il denaro
eel denaroh
money

il tasso di cambio
eel tassoh dee kambyo
exchange rate

Do I have...	Devo... *devoh*
...to key in my PIN?	...digitare il PIN? *deejeetareh eel peen*
...to sign here?	...firmare qui? *feermareh kwee*
The cash machine has taken my card	Lo sportello bancomat ha preso la mia carta *loh sportelloh bankomat ah presoh lah meea kartah*
Can I cash a cheque?	Posso incassare un assegno? *possoh eenkassareh oon assenyo*
Has my money arrived yet?	È arrivato il mio denaro? *eh arreevatoh eel meeo denaroh*
When does the bank open/close?	Quando apre/chiude la banca? *kwandoh apreh/kewdeh lah bankah*

lo sportello
bancomat
*loh sportelloh
bancomat*
cash machine

la carta di credito
*lah kartah dee
kredeetoh*
credit card

il libretto
degli assegni
*eel leebrettoh
delyee assenyee*
cheque book

SHOPS

il fruttivendolo
eel frooteevendoloh
greengrocer's

la pescheria
lah peskerya
fishmonger

la drogheria
lah drogerya
grocer's

la gastronomia
lah gastronomya
delicatessen

la panetteria
lah panetterya
baker's

la libreria
lah leebrerya
book shop

il supermercato
eel soopermerkatoh
supermarket

la macelleria
lah machelerya
butcher's

il tabaccaio
eel tabakkayo
tobacconist

il negozio di mobili
eel negotsyo dee mobeelee
furniture shop

il negozio di calzature
eel negotsyo dee kaltsatooreh
shoe shop

la boutique
lah booteek
boutique

la sartoria
lah sartorya
tailor's

la gioielleria
lah joyellerya
jeweller's

la ferramenta
lah ferramentah
hardware shop

AT THE MARKET

I would like...	Desidero... *deseederoh*
How much is this?	Quanto costa? *kwantoh kostah*
What's the price per kilo?	Quanto costa al chilo? *kwantoh kostah al keeloh*
It's too expensive	È troppo caro *eh troppoh karoh*
Do you have anything cheaper?	Avete qualcosa di meno caro? *aveteh kwalkosah dee menoh karoh*
That's fine, I'll take it	Va bene, lo prendo *vah beneh loh prendoh*
I'll take two kilos	Me ne dia due chili *meh neh dya dooeh keelee*
A kilo of...	Un chilo di... *oon keeloh dee*
Half a kilo of...	Mezzo chilo di... *medzo keeloh dee*
A little more, please	Un po' di più, per favore *oon poh dee pew pehr favoreh*
May I taste it?	Posso assaggiarlo/a? *possoh assadjarloh/ah*
That will be all, thank you	È tutto, la ringrazio *eh tootoh lah reengratsyo*

YOU MAY HEAR...

Posso aiutarla?
possoh ayewtarlah
Can I help you?

Quanto ne vuole?
kwantoh neh vwoleh
How much would you like?

IN THE SUPERMARKET

Where is/are...
Dov'è/dove sono...
doveh/doveh sonoh

...the frozen foods
...i surgelati?
ee soorjelatee

...the drinks aisle?
...la corsia delle bibite?
lah korsya delleh beebeeteh

...the check-out?
...la cassa?
lah kassah

I'm looking for...
Sto cercando...
stoh cherkandoh

il carrello
eel karrelloh
trolley

il cestino
eel chesteenoh
basket

Do you have any more?
Ne avete ancora?
neh aveteh ankorah

Is this reduced?
È scontato?
eh skontatoh

Where do I pay?
Dove posso pagare?
doveh possoh pagareh

Shall I key in my PIN?
Devo digitare il PIN?
devoh deejeetareh eel peen

Can I have a bag?
Posso avere un sacchetto?
possoh avereh oon sakettoh

FRUIT

l'arancia
laranchya
orange

il limone
eel leemoneh
lemon

la pesca
lah peskah
peach

la pescanoce
lah peskanocheh
nectarine

il limone verde
*eel leemoneh
verdeh*
lime

la ciliegia
lah cheelyeja
cherries

l'albicocca
lalbeekokkah
apricot

la prugna
lah proonya
plum

il pompelmo
eel pompelmoh
grapefruit

il mirtillo
eel meerteeloh
blueberry

la fragola
la fragolah
strawberry

il lampone
eel lamponeh
raspberry

il melone
eel meloneh
melon

l'uva
loovah
grapes

la banana
lah bananah
banana

la melagrana
lah melagranah
pomegranate

la mela
lah melah
apple

la pera
lah perah
pear

l'ananas
lananas
pineapple

il mango
eel mangoh
mango

VEGETABLES

la patata
lah patatah
potato

la carota
lah karotah
carrot

il peperone
eel peperoneh
pepper

il peperoncino
eel peperoncheenoh
chilli

la melanzana
lah melandzanah
aubergine

il pomodoro
eel pomodoroh
tomato

la cipolla
lah cheepolah
onion

l'aglio
lalyo
garlic

la cipollina
lah cheepoleenah
spring onion

il porro
eel porroh
leek

il fungo
eel foongoh
mushroom

la zucchina
lah dzookeenah
courgette

i piselli
ee peesellee
**garden
peas**

i fagiolini
ee fajoleenee
**French
beans**

il cetriolo
eel chetryoloh
cucumber

il sedano
eel sedanoh
celery

gli spinaci
lyee speenachee
spinach

il broccolo
eel brokkoloh
broccoli

la lattuga
lah latoogah
lettuce

il cavolo
eel kavoloh
cabbage

MEAT AND POULTRY

May I have...

...a slice of...?

...a piece of...?

Posso avere...
possoh avereh

...una fetta di...?
oonah fettah dee

...un pezzo di...?
oon pedzo dee

il prosciutto cotto
eel proshewtoh kottoh
cooked ham

la carne
tritata
*lah karneh
treetatah*
mince

la bistecca
lah beestekka
steak

il filetto
eel feelettoh
fillet

il prosciutto crudo
eel proshewtoh kroodoh
cured ham

il rognone
*eel
ronyoneh*
kidney

il pollo
eel polloh
chicken

il salame di
cinghiale
*eel salameh dee
cheengyaleh*
**wild boar
salami**

FISH AND SHELLFISH

la sogliola
lah solyolah
sole

eel calamaro
eel kalamaroh
squid

il merluzzo
eel merloodzo
cod

la spigola
lah speegolah
sea bass

il sarago
eel saragoh
sea bream

la sardina
lah sardeenah
sardine

il granchio
eel grankyo
crab

l'aragosta
laragostah
lobster

la capasanta
lah kapasantah
scallop

il gambero
eel gamberoh
prawn

BREAD AND CAKES

il pane casalingo
eel paneh kasaleengoh
home-baked bread

il pan marino
eel pan mareenoh
rosemary bread

i grissini
ee greeseenee
breadsticks

il panino
eel paneenoh
roll

il cornetto
eel kornettoh
croissant

la focaccia
lah fokatchya
foccaccia

il panettone
eel panettoneh
panettone

il panforte
eel panforteh
panforte

**la crostata
al limone**
*lah krostatah
al leemoneh*
lemon tart

**la torta al
cioccolato**
*lah tortah al
chokolatoh*
chocolate cake

DAIRY PRODUCE

il latte intero
eel lateh eenteroh
whole milk

parzialmente scremato
partsyalmenteh skrematoh
semi-skimmed milk

lo yoghurt
loh yogoort
yoghurt

il burro
eel booroh
butter

la panna
lah pannah
single cream

la ricotta
lah reekottah
ricotta

il parmigiano
eel parmeejanoh
Parmesan cheese

la mozzarella
lah modzarellah
mozzarella

il provolone
eel provoloneh
Provolone

il pecorino
eel pekoreenoh
Pecorino

NEWSPAPERS AND MAGAZINES

Do you have...	Avete...
	aveteh
...a book of stamps?	...un carnet di francobolli?
	oon karneh dee frankobollee
...airmail stamps?	...francobolli di posta aerea?
	frankobollee dee postah ahehrehah
...a packet of envelopes?	...una confezione di buste?
	oonah konfetsyoneh dee boosteh
...some sticky tape?	... del nastro adesivo?
	del nastroh adeseevoh

la cartolina
lah kartoleenah
postcard

la matita
lah mateetah
pencil

i francobolli
ee frankobolee
stamps

la penna
lah pennah
pen

YOU MAY HEAR...

Quale desidera?
kwaleh deseederah
Which would you like?

Mi può dire la sua età?
mee pwo deereh lah sooa etah
How old are you?

Ha la carta d'identità?
ah lah kartah deedenteetah
Do you have ID?

I'd like...

...a pack of cigarettes

...a box of matches

Vorrei...
vorray

...un pacchetto di sigarette
oon pakkettoh dee seegaretteh

...una scatola di cerini
oonah skatolah dee chereenee

i fumetti
ee foomettee
comic

l'accendino
latchendeenoh
lighter

le matite colorate
leh mateeteh kolorateh
colouring pencils

le gomme da masticare
leh gommeh dah masteekareh
chewing gum

le caramelle
leh karamelleh
sweets

del tabacco
del tabakkoh
tobacco

la rivista
lah reeveestah
magazine

il quotidiano
eel kwoteedyanoh
newspaper

BUYING CLOTHES AND SHOES

I am looking for...	Sto cercando... *stoh cherkandoh*
I am size...	Porto la taglia... *portoh lah talya*
Do you have this...	Avete questo/a... *aveteh kwestoh/ah*
...in my size?	...nella mia taglia? *nellah meeah talya*
...in small?	...in taglia piccola? *een talya peekolah*
...in medium?	...in taglia media? *een talya medya*
...in large?	...in taglia grande? *een talya grandeh*
...in other colours?	...in altri colori? *een altree koloree*
Can I try this on?	Posso provarlo/a? *possoh provarloh/ah*
It's...	È... *eh*
...too big	...troppo grande *troppoh grandeh*
...too small	...troppo piccolo/a *troppoh peekoloh/ah*
I need...	Ho bisogno di... *oh beezonyo dee*
...a larger size	...una taglia più grande *oonah talya pew grandeh*
...a smaller size	...una taglia più piccola *oonah talya pew peekolah*
I'll take this one, please	Prendo questo/a, grazie *prendoh kwestoh/ah gratsye*

I take shoe size...	Mi serve un... *mee serveh oon*
Can I try...	Posso provare... *possoh provareh*
...this pair?	...questo paio? *kwestoh payo*
...those ones in the window?	...quelle in vetrina? *kwelleh een vetreenah*
These are...	Queste sono... *kwesteh sonoh*
...too tight	...troppo strette *troppoh stretteh*
...too big	...troppo larghe *troppoh largeh*
...too small	...troppo piccole *troppoh peekoleh*
...uncomfortable	...scomode *skomodeh*
Is there a bigger/smaller size?	Avete un numero più grande/piccolo? *aveteh oon noomeroh pew grandeh/peekoloh*

CLOTHES AND SHOE SIZES GUIDE

Women's clothes sizes										
UK	6	8	10	12	14	16	18	20		
Europe	34	36	38	40	42	44	46	48		

Men's clothes sizes										
UK	36	38	40	42	44	46	48	50		
Europe	46	48	50	52	54	56	58	60		

Shoe sizes										
UK	3	4	5	6	7	8	9	10	11	
Europe	36	37	38	39	40	42	43	45	46	

CLOTHES AND SHOES

il vestito
eel vesteetoh
dress

l'abito da sera
labeetoh dah serah
evening dress

la giacca
lah jakkah
jacket

il maglione
eel malyoneh
jumper

i jeans
ee jeens
jeans

la gonna
lah gonnah
skirt

la scarpa da ginnastica
lah skarpah dah jeennasteekah
trainers

lo stivale
loh steevaleh
boots

la borsa
lah borzah
handbag

la cintura
lah cheentoorah
belt

il vestito da
uomo
*eel vesteetoh
dah womoh*
suit

il cappotto
eel kapottoh
coat

la camicia
lah kameechya
shirt

la t-shirt
lah t-shirt
t-shirt

i calzoncini
*ee
kaltsoncheenee*
shorts

il sandalo
eel sandaloh
sandal

la scarpa
con lacci
*lah skarpah
kon latchee*
**lace-up
shoe**

la scarpa col
tacco alto
*lah skarpah kol
takko altoh*
**high-heeled
shoe**

l'infradito
leenfradeetoh
flip-flop

i calzini
ee kalseenee
socks

AT THE GIFT SHOP

I'd like to buy a gift for...	Vorrei acquistare un regalo per... *vorray akweestareh oon regaloh pehr*
...my mother/father	...mia madre/mio padre *meeah madreh/meeoh padreh*
...my daughter/son	...mia figlia/mio figlio *meeah feelya/meeoh feelyo*
...a child	...un/a bambino/a *oon/ah bambeenoh/ah*
...a friend	...un/a amico/a *oon/ah ameekoh/ah*
Can you recommend something?	Mi può consigliare qualcosa? *mee pwo konseelyareh kwalkosah*
Do you have a box for it?	Ha la scatola? *ah lah skatolah*
Can you gift-wrap it?	Può fare un pacchetto regalo? *pwo fareh oon pakettoh regaloh*

il bracciale
eel bratchyaleh
bracelet

i gemelli
ee jemellee
cufflinks

la collana
lah kollanah
necklace

l'orologio
lorolojoh
watch

il portafoglio
eel portafolyo
wallet

la bambola
lah bambolah
doll

il peluche
eel peloosh
soft toy

ı cıoccolatini
ee chokolateenee
chocolates

I want a souvenir of...	Desidero un souvenir di... *deseederoh oon soovenir dee*
Have you anything cheaper?	Ha qualcosa di meno caro? *ah kwalkosah dee menoh karoh*
Is there a guarantee?	È coperto/a da garanzia? *eh kopertoh/ah dah garantsya*

YOU MAY HEAR...

È un regalo?
eh oon regaloh
Is it a present?

Vuole un pacchetto regalo?
woleh oon pakettoh regaloh
Shall I gift-wrap it?

PHOTOGRAPHY

I'd like this film developed	Vorrei sviluppare questa pellicola *vorray sveeloopareh kwestah pelleekolah*
Do you have an express service?	Avete un servizio espresso? *aveteh oon serveetsyo espressoh*
Does it cost more?	Costa di più? *kostah dee pew*
I'd like...	Vorrei... *vorray*
...the one-hour service	...lo sviluppo in un'ora *loh sveeloopoh een oonorah*

la fotocamera
digitale
*lah fotokamerah
deejeetaleh*
digital camera

la scheda di memoria
*lah skedah dee
memorya*
memory card

la cornice
lah korneeche
photo frame

l'album delle fotografie
lalboom delleh fotografye
photo album

...a battery

...una batteria
oonah battereeya

Can you print from
this memory stick?

Potete stampare da questa
chiavetta USB?
*poteteh stampareh dah kwestah
kyakettah oo-es-bee*

gli obiettivi
lyee obyeteevee
lens

la fotocamera
lah fotokamerah
camera

la borsa per
fotocamera
*lah borsah pehr
fotokamerah*
camera bag

il flash
eel flash
flash gun

YOU MAY HEAR...

Quale formato di foto
desidera?
*kwaleh formatoh
deseedeerah*
**What size prints do
you want?**

Opache o lucide?
opakeh oh loocheedeh?
Matt or gloss?

AT THE POST OFFICE

I'd like...

Vorrei...
vorray

...three stamps, please

...tre francobolli, per favore
treh frankobollee pehr favoreh

...to register this letter

...inviare una raccomandata
eenvyareh oonah rakomandatah

...to send this airmail

...inviare questo per posta aerea
eenvyareh kwestoh pehr postah ahehreha

i francobolli
ee frankobollee
stamps

la busta
lah boostah
envelope

la posta aerea
lah postah ahehreha
airmail

la cartolina
lah kartoleenah
postcard

YOU MAY HEAR...

Cosa contiene?
kozah kontyeneh
What are the contents?

Qual è il suo valore?
kwaleh eel soo-oh valoreh
What is their value?

Riempia questo modulo
ryempya kwestoh modooloh
Fill out this form

How much is...?	Quanto costa... *kwantoh kostah*
...a letter to...	...una lettera per... *oonah letterah pehr*
...a postcard to...	...una cartolina per... *oonah kartoleenah pehr*
...the United States	...gli Stati Uniti *lyee statee ooneetee*
...Great Britain	...la Gran Bretagna *lah gran bretanya*
...Canada	...il Canada *eel kanadah*
...Australia	...l'Australia *lowstralya*
Can I have a receipt?	Posso avere la ricevuta? *possoh avereh lah reechevootah*
Where can I post this?	Dove posso imbucare questa lettera? *doveh possoh eembookareh kwestah letterah*

il pacco
eel pakoh
parcel

il corriere
eel korryereh
courier

la cassetta delle lettere
lah kassettah delleh lettereh
postbox

il postino
eel posteenoh
postman

TELEPHONES

Where is the nearest phone shop?	Dove è il negozio di telefoni più vicino? *Doveh eel negotsyo dee telehfonee pew veecheenoh*
Who's speaking?	Pronto, chi parla? *prontoh kee parlah*
Hello, this is...	Pronto, sono... *prontoh sonoh*
I'd like to speak to...	Vorrei parlare con... *vorray parlareh kon*

il telefono
eel telefonoh
phone

lo smartphone
loh smartphone
smartphone

il cellulare
eel chelloolareh
mobile phone

la segreteria telefonica
lah segreterya telefoneekah
answering machine

il telefono a moneta
eel telefonoh ah monetah
coin phone

INTERNET

Is there an internet café near here?

C'è un Internet cafè qui vicino?
che oon eenternet kafeh kwee veecheenoh

How much do you charge?

Quanto costa?
kwantoh kostah

Do you have wireless internet?

Avete un sistema Internet wireless?
aveteh oon seestemah eenternet wireless

Can I check my emails?

Posso controllare le mie e-mail?
possoh kontrollareh leh meeyeh emayl

I need to send an email

Devo inviare un'e-mail
devoh eenvyareh oonemayl

What's your email address?

Qual è il suo indirizzo e-mail?
kwaleh eel soo-oh eendeereedzo emayl

My email address is...

Il mio indirizzo e-mail è...
eel meeoh eendeereedzo emayl eh

il computer portatile
eel compewter portateeleh
laptop

la tastiera
lah tastyerah
keyboard

il sito Web
eel seetoh web
website

l'e-mail
lemayl
email

SIGHTSEEING

Most Italian cities and towns have a tourist information
office, which is usually situated near the railway station
or town hall. The staff will advise you on local places of
interest to visit and cultural events. In Italy, most national
museums close on Mondays as well as on public holidays,
so make sure that you check the opening times
before visiting.

AT THE TOURIST OFFICE

Where is the tourist
information office?

Dov'è l'ufficio del turismo?
doveh loofeechyo del tooreesmoh

Can you recommend...

Può consigliarmi...
pwo konseelyarmee

...a guided tour?

...una visita guidata?
oonah veeseetah gweedatah

...an excursion?

...una gita?
oonah jeetah

Is there a museum or
art gallery?

C'è un museo o una galleria
d'arte?
*che oon moozeoh oh oonah
gallereeya darteh*

Is it open to the public?

È aperto/a al pubblico?
eh apertoh/ah al poobleekoh

Is there wheelchair
access?

C'è un accesso per disabili?
che oon atchessoh pehr deezabeelee

Does it close...

È chiuso/a...
eh kewsoh/ah

...on Sundays?

...la domenica?
lah domeneekah

...on bank holidays?

...nei giorni festivi?
nay jornee festeevee

How long does it take to
get there?

Quanto ci vuole per arrivarci?
*kwantoh chee vwoleh pehr
areevarchee*

Do you have...

Avete...
aveteh

...a street map?

...una cartina?
oonah karteenah

...a guide?

...una guida?
oonah gweedah

...any leaflets?

...degli opuscoli?
dehlyee opooskolee

VISITING PLACES

What time...	A che ora... *ah ke orah*
...do you open?	...apre? *apreh*
...do you close?	...chiude? *kewdeh*
I'd like two entrance tickets	Vorrei due biglietti d'entrata *vorray dooeh beelyettee dentratah*
Two adults, please	Due adulti, per favore *dooeh adooltee pehr favoreh*
A family ticket	Un biglietto famiglia *oon beelyettoh fameelya*
How much does it cost?	Quanto costa? *kwantoh kostah*
Are there reductions for...	Ci sono delle riduzioni per... *chee sonoh delleh reedootsyonee pehr*
...children?	...i bambini? *ee bambeenee*
...students?	...gli studenti? *lyee stoodentee*

la pianta della città
lah pyantah dellah cheetah
street map

il biglietto d'entrata
eel beelyettoh dentratah
entrance ticket

l'ufficio del turismo
loofeechyo del tooreesmol
tourist office

l'accesso disabili
latchessoh deezabeele
wheelchair access

Can I buy a guidebook?	Posso acquistare una guida? *possoh akweestareh oonah gweedah*
Is there...	C'è... *che*
...an audio-guide?	...un'audio guida? *oonowdyo gweedah*
...a guided tour?	...una visita guidata? *oonah veeseetah gweedatah*
...a lift?	...un ascensore? *oon ashenzoreh*
...a bus tour?	...un giro turistico in autobus? *oon jeeroh tooreesteeko een owtoboos*
When is the next tour?	Quando parte il prossimo giro turistico? *kwandoh parteh eel proseemoh jeeroh tooreesteeko*

il tour in autobus
eel tour een owtoboos
tour bus

YOU MAY HEAR...

Quanti anni ha?   Possiede una carta studenti?
kwantee annee ah   *possyedeh oonah kartah stoodentee*
How old are you? **Do you have a student card?**

FINDING YOUR WAY

Excuse me	Mi scusi
	mee skoozee
Can you help me?	Mi può aiutare?
	mee pwo ayewtareh
Is this the way to...?	È questa la strada per...?
	eh kwestah lah stradah pehr
How do I get to...?	Come raggiungo...?
	komeh radjewngoh
...the town centre?	...il centro della città?
	eel chentroh dellah cheetah
...the station?	...la stazione?
	lah statsyoneh
...the museum?	...il museo?
	eel moozeoh
...the art gallery?	...la galleria d'arte?
	lah gallereeya darteh
How long does it take?	Quanto tempo s'impiega?
	kwantoh tempoh seempyegah
Is it far?	È lontano?
	eh lontanoh
Can you show me on the map?	Me lo può indicare sulla cartina?
	meh loh pwo eendeekareh soolah karteenah

YOU MAY HEAR...

Non è lontano
non eh lontanoh
It's not far away

Ci vogliono dieci minuti
chee volyonoh deeaychee meenootee
It takes ten minutes.

YOU MAY HEAR...

Siamo qui
syamoh kwee
We are here

Vada sempre dritto...
vadah sempreh dreetoh
Keep straight on...

...fino alla fine della via
feenoh allah feeneh dellah veeya
...to the end of the street

...fino al semaforo
feenoh al semaforoh
...to the traffic lights

...fino alla piazza principale
feenoh allah pyadza preencheepaleh
...to the main square

Di qua
dee kwa
This way

Di là
dee lah
That way

Svolti a destra al/alla...
svoltee ah destrah al/allah
Turn right at...

Svolti a sinistra al/alla...
svoltee ah seeneestrah al/allah
Turn left at...

Prenda la prima...
prendah lah preemah
Take the first...

...a sinistra/a destra
ah seeneestrah/ah destrah
...on the left/right

È davanti a lei
eh davantee ah lay
It's in front of you

È dietro di lei
eh deeyehtroh dee lay
It's behind you

È di fronte a lei
eh dee fronteh ah lay
It's opposite you

È vicino a...
eh veecheenoh ah
It's next to...

C'è un'indicazione
che ooneendeekatsyoneh
It's signposted

È là
eh lah
It's over there

PLACES TO VISIT

il municipio
eel mooneecheepyo
town hall

il ponte
eel ponteh
bridge

il museo
eel moozeoh
museum

la galleria d'arte
lah gallereeya darteh
art gallery

il monumento
eel monoomentoh
monument

la chiesa
lah kyezah
church

il paese
eel paheseh
village

la cattedrale
lah katedraleh
cathedral

il castello
eel kastelloh
castle

il faro
eel faroh
lighthouse

il porto
eel portoh
harbour

il vigneto
eel veenyetoh
vineyard

il parco
eel parkoh
park

la costa
lah kostah
coast

la cascata
lah kaskatah
waterfall

le montagne
leh montanye
mountains

OUTDOOR ACTIVITIES

Where can we go...	Dove possiamo... *doveh possyamoh*
...horse riding?	...andare a cavallo? *andareh ah kavalloh*
...fishing?	...andare a pescare? *andareh ah peskareh*
...swimming?	...nuotare? *nwotareh*
...walking?	...fare un'escursione a piedi? *fareh oon eskoorzyoneh ah pyedee*
Can we...	Possiamo... *possyamoh*
...hire equipment?	...noleggiare l'attrezzatura? *noledjareh lattredzatoorah*
...have lessons?	...prendere delle lezioni? *prendereh delleh letsyonee*
How much per hour?	Quanto costa all'ora? *kwantoh kostah allorah*
I'm a beginner	Sono un/a principiante *sonoh oon/ah preencheepyanteh*
I'm very experienced	Ho una buona esperienza *Oh oonah bwonah esperyentsah*
Where's the amusement park?	Dov'è il parco dei divertimenti? *doveh eel parkoh day deeverteementee*
Can the children go on all the rides?	I bambini possono andare su tutte le giostre? *ee bambeenee possonoh andareh soo tooteh leh jostreh*
Is there a playground?	C'è un'area giochi? *che oon ahrehah jokee*
Is it safe for children?	È sicura per i bambini? *eh seekoorah pehr ee bambeenee*

lo zoo
loh dzoh
zoo

l'area giochi
larehah jokee
playground

il picnic
eel picnic
picnic

il luna park
eel loonah park
fairground

pescare
peskareh
fishing

andare a cavallo
andareh ah kavalloh
horse riding

il parco safari
eel parkoh safaree
safari park

il parco a tema
eel parkoh ah temah
theme park

SPORTS AND LEISURE

Italy can offer the traveller a wide range of cultural events, entertainments, leisure activities and sports. The Italians are proud of their rich artistic and musical heritage, and their distinctive culture is very important to them. For the sports enthusiast, a wide range of spectator sports and facilities are available, from winter sports, climbing and hiking in the Alps and Appenines to watersports around the coast and on inland lakes. Football is the national game and you can watch a *Serie* A match.

LEISURE TIME

I like...
Mi piace/piacciono...
mee pyaceh/pyatchyonoh

...art and painting
...l'arte e la pittura
larteh eh lah peetoorah

...films and cinema
...i film e il cinema
ee film eh eel cheenemah

...the theatre
...il teatro
eel tehatroh

...opera
...l'opera
loperah

I prefer...
Preferisco...
prefereeskoh

...reading books
...leggere libri
ledjereh leebree

...listening to music
...ascoltare musica
askoltareh moozeekah

...watching sport
...guardare lo sport
gwardareh loh sport

...going to concerts
...andare ai concerti
andareh ahee konchertee

...dancing
...ballare
ballareh

...going clubbing
...andare in discoteca
andareh een deeskotekah

...going out with friends
...uscire con gli amici
oosheereh kon lyee ameechee

I don't like...
Non mi piace...
non mee pyacheh

That doesn't interest me
Non mi interessa
non mee eenteressah

AT THE BEACH

Can I hire...	Posso noleggiare... *possoh noledjareh*
...a jet ski?	...una moto d'acqua? *oonah motoh dakwa*
...a beach umbrella?	...un ombrellone da mare? *oon ombrelloneh dah mareh*
...a surfboard?	...una tavola da surf? *oonah tavolah dah surf*
...a wetsuit?	...una muta subacquea? *oonah mootah soobakweah*

il telo da mare
eel teloh dah mareh
beach towel

la sedia a sdraio
lah sedya ah sdrayo
deck chair

il pallone da spiaggia
eel palloneh dah speeadjah
beach ball

il lettino sdraio
eel leteenoh sdrayo
sun lounger

YOU MAY HEAR...

Divieto di balneazione
deevyetoh dee balneatsyoneh
No swimming

Spiaggia chiusa
speeadja kewsah
Beach closed

How much does it cost?	Quanto costa? *kwantoh kostah*
Can I go water-skiing?	Posso fare dello sci d'acqua? *possoh fareh delloh shee dakwa*
Is there a lifeguard?	C'è il bagnino? *che eel baneenoh*
Is it safe to...	È sicuro... *eh seekooroh*
...swim here?	...nuotare qui? *nwotareh kwee*
...surf here?	...fare del surf qui? *fareh del surf kwee*

gli occhiali da sole
lyee okeealee dah soleh
sunglasses

il cappello da sole
eel kappeloh dah soleh
sunhat

le pinne
leh peenneh
flippers

la lozione solare
lah lotsyoneh solareh
suntan lotion

il bikini
eel beekeenee
bikini

la maschera e il boccaglio
lah maskerah eh eel bokalyo
mask and snorkel

AT THE SWIMMING POOL

What time...

Quando...
kwandoh

...does the pool open?

...apre la piscina?
apreh lah peesheenah

...does the pool close?

...chiude la piscina?
kewdeh lah peesheenah

Is it...

È...
eh

...an indoor pool?

...una piscina coperta?
oonah peesheenah kopertah

...an outdoor pool?

...una piscina all'aperto?
oonah peesheenah alapertoh

Is there a children's pool?

C'è una piscina per bambini?
che oonah peesheenah pehr bambeenee

Where are the changing rooms?

Dove sono gli spogliatoi?
doveh sonoh lyee spolyatoy

Is it safe to dive?

È sicuro tuffarsi?
eh seekooroh toofarsee

i braccioli
ee bratchyolee
armband

la tavoletta
lah tavolettah
float

gli occhialini
lyee okyaleenee
swimming goggles

il costume
eel kostoomeh
swimsuit

AT THE GYM

l'ellittica
lelleeteekah
cross trainer

la bicicletta
lah beecheeklettah
exercise bike

il vogatore
eel vogatoreh
rowing machine

la step machine
lah step machine
step machine

Is there a gym?	C'è una palestra? *che oonah palestrah*
Is it free for guests?	È gratuita per i clienti? *eh gratooeetah pehr ee klyentee*
Do I have to wear trainers?	Devo indossare le scarpe da ginnastica? *devoh eendossareh leh skarpeh dah jeennasteekah*
Do I need an induction session?	Devo fare una sessione introduttiva? *devoh fareh oonah sessyoneh introdootteevah*
Do you hold...	Offrite... *offreeteh*
...aerobics classes?	...lezioni di aerobica? *letsyonee dee aerobeekah*
...Pilates classes?	...lezioni di Pilates? *letsyonee dee pilates*
...yoga classes?	...lezioni di yoga? *letsyonee dee yogah*

BOATING AND SAILING

Can I hire...	Posso noleggiare... *possoh noledjareh*
...a dinghy?	...un gommone? *oon gommoneh*
...a windsurfer?	...una tavola da windsurf? *oonah tavolah dah windsurf*
...a canoe?	...una canoa? *oonah kanoah*
Do you offer sailing lessons?	Offrite lezioni di vela? *offreeteh letsyonee dee velah*
Do you have a mooring?	Avete un ormeggio? *aveteh oon ormedjoh*
How much is it for the night?	Quanto costa per notte? *kwantoh kostah pehr notteh*
Where can I buy gas?	Dove posso acquistare del gasolio? *doveh possoh akweestareh del gazolyo*
Where is the marina?	Dov'è il porticciolo? *doveh eel porteetchyoloh*
My...is broken	Il mio/la mia...non funziona *eel meeoh/lah meeah...non foontsyonah*
Can you repair it?	Potete ripararlo/a? *poteteh reepararloh/ah*
Are there life jackets?	Ci sono dei giubbotti di salvataggio? *chee sonoh day jewbottee dee salvatadjoh*

il giubbotto di salvataggio
eel jewbottoh dee salvatadjoh
life jacket

la bussola
lah boosolah
compass

WINTER SPORTS

I would like to hire...	Desidero noleggiare... *deseederoh noledjareh*
...some skis	...un paio di sci *oon payo dee shee*
...some ski boots	...un paio di scarponi *oon payo dee skarponee*
...some poles	...un paio di racchette *oon payo dee raketteh*
...a snowboard	...uno snowboard *oonoh snowboard*
...a helmet	...un casco *oon kaskoh*
When does...	Quando... *kwandoh*
...the chair lift start?	...apre la seggiovia? *apreh lah sedjoveeya*
...the cable car finish?	...chiude la funivia? *kewdeh lah fooneeveeya*
How much is a lift pass?	Quanto costa un pass? *kwantoh kostah oon pass*
Can I take skiing lessons?	Posso prendere delle lezioni di sci? *possoh prendereh delleh letsyonee dee shee*

YOU MAY HEAR...

È un principiante?
eh oon preencheepeeeanteh
Are you a beginner?

Deve lasciare un deposito
deveh lashyareh oon deposeetoh
I need a deposit

BALL GAMES

I like playing...	Mi piace giocare a... *mee pyacheh jokareh ah*
...football	...pallone *palloneh*
...tennis	...tennis *tennis*
...golf	...golf *golf*
...badminton	...volano *volahnoh*
...squash	...squash *skwosh*
...baseball	...baseball *besboll*
Where is the nearest...	Dov'è il più vicino... *doveh eel pew veecheenoh*
...tennis court?	...campo da tennis? *kampoh dah tennis*
...golf course?	...campo da golf? *kampoh dah golf*
...sports centre?	...centro sportivo? *chentroh sporteevoh*

il pallone
eel palloneh
football

il canestro
eel kanestroh
basket

il guanto da baseball
eel gwantoh dah besball
baseball mitt

Can I book a court...	Posso prenotare un campo... *possoh prenotareh oon kampoh*
...for two hours?	...per due ore? *pehr dooeh oreh*
...at three o'clock?	...per le tre? *pehr leh tray*
What shoes are allowed?	Quali scarpe sono permesse? *kwalee skarpeh sonoh permesseh*
Can I hire...	Posso noleggiare... *possoh noledjareh*
...a tennis racquet?	...una racchetta da tennis? *oonah rakettah dah tennis*
...some balls?	...delle palle? *delleh palleh*
...a set of clubs?	...un set di mazze? *oon set dee madze*
...a golf buggy?	...il carrello elettrico? *eel karreloh elettreekoh*

le palle
leh palleh
tennis balls

la mazza
lah madza
golf club

i polsini
ee polseenee
wristbands

la palla e il tee
lah pallah eh eel tee
golf ball and tee

la racchetta
lah rakettah
tennis racquet

GOING OUT

Where is...	Dov'è... *doveh*
...the opera house?	...il teatro dell'opera? *eel teatroh delloperah*
...a jazz club?	...il jazz club? *eel jazz clab*
Do I have to book in advance?	Devo prenotare in anticipo? *devoh prenotareh een anteecheepoh*
I'd like...tickets	Vorrei...biglietti *vorray...beelyettee*
I'd like seats...	Vorrei dei posti... *vorray day postee*
...at the back	...in fondo *een fondoh*
...at the front	...davanti *davantee*
...in the middle	...nel mezzo *nel medzo*
...in the gallery	...in galleria *een gallereeya*
Can I buy a programme?	Posso acquistare un programma? *possoh akweestareh oon programmah*
Is there live music?	C'è musica dal vivo? *che moozeekah dal veevoh*

YOU MAY HEAR...

Spenga il cellulare
spengah eel chelloolareh
Turn off your mobile

Torni a sedere
tornee ah sedereh
Return to your seats

il musicista
eel noozeecheestah
musician

il teatro
eel teatroh
theatre

il teatro dell'opera
eel teatroh delloperah
opera house

la discoteca
lah deeskotehkah
nightclub

il/la cantante
eel/lah kantanteh
singer

il pianista
eel pyaneestah
pianist

il cinema
eel cheenemah
cinema

i popcorn
ee popcorn
popcorn

la danza
lah dandza
ballet

il casinò
eel kaseenoh
casino

GALLERIES AND MUSEUMS

What are the opening hours?
Qual è l'orario di apertura?
kwaleh loraryo dapertoorah

Are there guided tours in English?
Ci sono delle visite guidate in inglese?
chee sonoh delleh veezeeteh gweedateh een eenglezeh

When does the tour leave?
Quando inizia la visita?
kwandoh eeneetsya lah veezeetah

How much does it cost?
Quanto costa?
kwantoh kostah

How long does it take?
Quanto dura?
kwantoh doorah

Do you have an audio guide?
Avete delle guide audio?
aveteh delleh gweedeh owdyo

Do you have a guidebook in English?
Avete una guida in inglese?
aveteh oonah gweedah een eenglezeh

Can you direct me to...?
Mi può indirizzare a...?
mee pwo eendeereetsareh ah

Is (flash) photography allowed?
Sono permesse le fotografie (con il flash)?
sonoh permesseh leh fotografye (kon eel flash)

la statua
lah statwa
statue

il busto
eel boostoh
bust

d really like to see...   Mi piacerebbe molto visitare...
mee pyacherebbeh moltoh veezeetareh

/ho painted this?   Chi è l'autore di questo quadro?
ki eh lowtoreh dee kwestoh kwadroh

low old is it?   A quando risale?
ah kwandoh reesaleh

re there wheelchair ramps?   Ci sono delle rampe per disabili?
chee sonoh delleh rampeh pehr deezabeelee

there a lift?   C'è un ascensore?
che oon ashensoreh

/here are the toilets?   Dov'è la toilette?
doveh lah twalet

ve lost my group   Ho perso il mio gruppo
oh persoh eel meeoh grooppoh

il dipinto
eel deepeentoh
painting

il disegno
eel deesenyo
drawing

l'incisione
leencheesyoneh
engraving

il manoscritto
eel manoskreettoh
manuscript

HOME ENTERTAINMENT

How do I...	Come... *komeh*
...turn the television on?	...accendo il televisore? *atchendoh eel televeezoreh*
...change channels?	...cambio i canali? *kambyo ee kanalee*
...turn the volume up?	...alzo il volume? *altso eel voloomeh*
...turn the volume down?	...abbasso il volume? *abassoh eel voloomeh*
Do you have satellite TV?	Avete una TV satellitare? *aveteh oonah TV satelleetareh*
Where can I buy...	Dove posso acquistare... *doveh possoh akweestareh*
...a DVD?	...un DVD? *oon deeveedee*
...a music CD?	...un CD musicale? *oon cheedee moozeekaleh*
...an audio CD?	...un CD audio? *oon cheedee owdyo*

il televisore a schermo panoramico
eel televeezoreh ah skermoh panorameekoh
widescreen TV

il lettore DVD
eel lettoreh deeveedee
DVD player

il telecomando
eel telekomandoh
remote control

il videogioco
eel videojokoh
video game

l penna USB
lah pennah uh-es-bee
USB flash drive

il portatile
eel portateeleh
laptop

la radio
lah radyo
radio

l'hard drive
lard drive
hard drive

il mouse
eel mows
mouse

Can I use this to...	Posso usarlo per... *possoh oozarloh pehr*
...go online?	...accedere ad Internet? *atchedereh ad eenternet*
Is it broadband/wifi?	È a banda larga/wifi? *eh ah bandah largah/wifi*
How do I...	Come... *komeh*
...log on?	...mi conetto? *mee konnettoh*
...log out?	...mi disconetto? *mee deeskonnettoh*
...reboot?	...riavvio il computer? *reeyaveeyo eel compooter*

HEALTH

If you are an EU national, you are entitled to free emergency medical treatment in Italy, but you will have to produce your European Health Insurance Card. Otherwise, make sure your travel insurance policy covers you for medical treatment. It is a good idea to familiarize yourself with a few basic phrases for use in an emergency, or in case you need to go to a pharmacy, or visit a doctor, dentist or hospital

USEFUL PHRASES

I need a doctor	Ho bisogno di un medico *oh beezonyo dee oon medeekoh*
I would like an appointment...	Vorrei prendere un appuntamento... *vorray prendereh oon apoontamentoh*
...as soon as possible	...al più presto possibile *al pew prestoh posseebeeleh*
...today	...per oggi *pehr odjee*
...tomorrow	...per domani *pehr domanee*
It's very urgent	È molto urgente *eh moltoh oorjenteh*
I have a European Health Insurance Card	Possiedo una carta di assistenza sanitaria europea *possyedoh oonah kartah dee asseestentsa saneetarya ehooropayah*
I have health insurance	Ho un'assicurazione sanitaria *oh oon asseekooratsyoneh saneetarya*
Can I have a receipt?	Posso avere la ricevuta? *possoh avereh lah reechevootah*
Where is the nearest...	Dov'è la più vicino/a... *doveh lah pew veecheenoh/ah*
...pharmacy?	...farmacia? *farmacheeya*
...doctor's surgery?	...ambulatorio medico? *amboolatoryo medeekoh*
...hospital?	...ospedale? *ospedaleh*
...dentist?	...dentista? *denteestah*

AT THE PHARMACY

What can I take for...?	Cosa posso prendere per...? *kozah possoh prendereh pehr*
How many should I take?	Quante ne devo prendere? *kwanteh neh devoh prendereh*
Is it safe for children?	È sicuro/a per i bambini? *eh seekooroh/ah pehr ee bambeenee*
Are there side effects?	Ha degli effetti indesiderati? *ah delyee effetee eendeseederatee*
Do you have that...	Questo prodotto viene venduto... *kwestoh prodottoh vyeneh vendootoh*
...as tablets?	...in compresse? *een kompresseh*
...in capsule form?	...in capsule? *een kapsooleh*
I'm allergic to...	Sono allergico/a a... *sonoh allerjeekoh/ah ah*
I'm already taking...	Sto già prendendo... *stoh jah prendendoh*
Do I need a prescription?	Ho bisogno della ricetta medica? *oh beezonyo dellah reechettah medeekah*

YOU MAY HEAR...

Prenda questo/a... volte al giorno
prendah kwestoh/ah...volteh al jornoh
Take this...times a day

Durante i pasti
dooranteh ee pastee
With food

le bende
leh bendeh
bandage

il cerotto
eel cherottoh
plaster

le capsule
leh kapsooleh
capsules

le compresse
leh compresseh
pills

la pomata
lah pomatah
ointment

le supposte
leh soopposteh
suppositories

le gocce
leh goccheh
drops

l'inalatore
leenalatoreh
inhaler

lo spray
loh spry
spray

lo sciroppo
loh sheeroppoh
syrup

THE HUMAN BODY

I have hurt my...

Mi sono fatto/a male al/alla...
mee sonoh fattoh/ah maleh al/allah

il gomito
eel gomeetoh
elbow

il braccio
eel bratchyo
arm

la testa
lah testah
head

la spalla
lah spallah
shoulder

il collo
eel kolloh
neck

il torace
eel torache
chest

lo stomaco
loh stomakoh
stomach

la gamba
lah gambah
leg

il ginocchio
eel jeenokyo
knee

il piede
eel pyedeh
foot

FACE

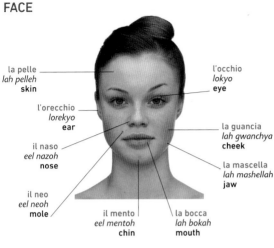

la pelle
lah pelleh
skin

l'occhio
lokyo
eye

l'orecchio
lorekyo
ear

la guancia
lah gwanchya
cheek

il naso
eel nazoh
nose

la mascella
lah mashellah
jaw

il neo
eel neoh
mole

il mento
eel mentoh
chin

la bocca
lah bokah
mouth

HAND

FOOT

l'unghia
loongya
nail

l'alluce
lalooche
toe

il dito
eel deetoh
finger

il pollice
eel polleeche
thumb

la caviglia
lah kaveelya
ankle

il polso
eel polsoh
wrist

il tallone
eel taloneh
heel

FEELING ILL

I don't feel well	Non mi sento bene
	non mee sentoh beneh
I feel ill	Mi sento male
	mee sentoh maleh
I have...	Ho...
	Oh
...an ear ache	...mal d'orecchio
	mal dorekyo
...a stomach ache	...mal di stomaco
	mal dee stomakoh
...a sore throat	...la gola infiammata
	lah golah enfyammatah
...a temperature	...la febbre
	lah febbreh
...hayfever	...il raffreddore da fieno
	eel rafreddoreh dah fyenoh
...constipation	...costipazione
	kosteepatsyoneh
...diarrhoea	...diarrea
	dyareah
...toothache	...mal di denti
	mal dee dentee
I've been stung by...	Mi ha punto...
	mee ah poontoh
...a bee/wasp	...un'ape/una vespa
	oonapeh/oonah vespah
...a jellyfish	...una medusa
	oonah medoosah
I've been bitten by...	Mi ha morso...
	mee ah morsoh
...a dog	...un cane
	oon kaneh

INJURIES

il morso
eel morsoh
bite

la puntura
lah poontoorah
sting

la frattura
lah fratoorah
fracture

l'escoriazione
leskoryatsyoneh
graze

la scheggia
lah skedjah
splinter

la bruciatura
lah broochyatoorah
burn

il taglio
eel talyo
cut

l'ematoma
lematomah
bruise

la scottatura solare
lah skotatoorah solareh
sunburn

la distorsione
lah deestorsyoneh
sprain

AT THE DOCTOR

I'm...
Sto...
stoh

...vomiting
...vomitando
vomeetandoh

...bleeding
...perdendo sangue
perdendoh sangwe

...dizzy
...ho le vertigini
oh leh verteejeenee

...feeling faint
...mi sento svenire
mee sentoh sveneereh

...pregnant
...sono incinta
sonoh eencheentah

...diabetic
...ho il diabete
oh eel dyabeteh

...epileptic
...sono epilettico/a
sonoh epeeletteekoh/ah

I have...
Soffro di...
soffroh dee

...arthritis
...artrite
artreeteh

...a heart condition
...una patologia cardiaca
oonah patolojeea kardeeakah

...high blood pressure
...elevata pressione sanguigna
elevatah pressyoneh sangweenya

YOU MAY HEAR...

Cosa c'è che non va?
kozah che ke non vah
What's wrong?

Dove le fa male?
doveh leh fah maleh
Where does it hurt?

Posso visitarla?
possoh veezeetarlah
Can I examine you?

ILLNESS

la tosse
lah tosseh
cough

l'asma
lasmah
asthma

il raffreddore
eel rafreddoreh
cold

l'influenza
leenflooentsa
flu

lo starnuto
loh starnootoh
sneeze

i crampi
ee krampee
stomach cramps

la nausea
lah nowzeah
nausea

l'eruzione cutanea
lerootsyoneh kootaneah
rash

il sangue dal naso
eel sangwe dal nasoh
nosebleed

il mal di testa
eel mal dee testah
headache

AT THE HOSPITAL

Can you help me?	Mi può aiutare? *mee pwo ayewtareh*
I need...	Ho bisogno di... *oh beezonyo dee*
...a doctor	...un dottore *oon dottoreh*
...a nurse	...un'infermiera *oon eenfermyerah*
Where is...	Dov'è... *doveh*
...the accident and emergency department?	...il Pronto Soccorso? *eel prontoh sokorsoh*
...the children's ward?	...il reparto pediatrico? *eel repartoh pedyatreeko*
...the X-ray department?	...il reparto di radiologia? *eel repartoh dee radyolojah*
...the lift/stairs?	...l'ascensore/la scala? *lashensoreh/lah skalah*

l'iniezione
leenyetsyoneh
injection

la radiografia
lah radyografya
X-ray

le analisi
del sangue
*leh analeezee
del sangwe*
blood test

l'ecografia,
la TAC
*lekografya
lah tac*
scan

...the waiting room?	...la sala d'attesa? *lah salah dattezah*
...the intensive care unit?	...il reparto di terapia intensiva? *eel repartoh dee terapya eentenseevah*
I think I've broken...	Penso di essermi rotto/a... *pensoh dee essermee rottoh/ah*
Do I need...	Ho bisogno di... *oh beezonyo dee*
...an injection?	...un'iniezione? *ooneenyetsyoneh*
...an operation?	...un'operazione? *oonoperatsyoneh*
Will it hurt?	Sarà doloroso/a? *sarah dolorozoh/ah*
How long will it take?	Quanto tempo sarà necessario? *kwantoh tempoh sarah nechessaryo*
What are the visiting hours?	Quali sono gli orari di visita? *kwalee sonoh lyee oraree dee veezeetah*

la rianimazione
lah reeaneematsyoneh
resuscitation

la sedia a rotelle
lah sedya ah rotelleh
wheelchair

la stecca
lah stekkah
splint

la fasciatura
lah fashyatoorah
dressing

EMERGENCIES

In an emergency, you should dial 112 and ask for either an ambulance (*un ambulanza*), the fire brigade (*i vigili del fuoco*), the police (*la Polizia*) or the military police (*i Carabinieri*), which is part of the army. If you are the victim of a crime or lose your passport and money, you should report the incident to the police. In the following pages, you will find some useful phrases to help you.

IN AN EMERGENCY

Help!
Aiuto!
ayewtoh

Please go away!
Mi lasci stare!
mee lashee stareh

Let go!
Lasci!
lashee

Stop! Thief!
Fermo! Al ladro!
fermoh al ladroh

Call the police!
Chiamate la polizia!
kiamateh lah poleetseeya

Get a doctor!
Trovate un dottore!
trovateh oon dottoreh

I need...
Ho bisogno...
oh beezonyo

...the police
...della polizia
dellah poleetseeya

...the fire brigade
...dei vigili del fuoco
day veejeelee del fwoko

...an ambulance
...di un'ambulanza
dee oon amboolantsa

It's very urgent
È molto urgente
eh moltoh oorjenteh

Where is...
Dov'è...
doveh

...the American/British embassy?
...l'ambasciata americana/brittanica?
lambashyatah amereekanah/breetaneekah

...the police station?
...il commissariato?
eel komeesareeyatoh

...the hospital?
...l'ospedale?
lospedaleh

ACCIDENTS

| I need to make a telephone call | Devo fare una telefonata
devoh fareh oonah telefonatah |
| I'd like to report an accident | Vorrei denunciare un incidente
vorray denoonchyareh oon eencheedenteh |
| I've crashed my car | Ho avuto un incidente d'auto
oh avootoh oon eencheedenteh dowtoh |
| The registration number is... | Il numero di targa è...
eel noomeroh dee targah eh |
| I'm at... | Mi trovo a/in...
mee trovoh ah/een |
| Please come quickly! | Venite subito, per favore!
veneeteh soobeetoh pehr favoreh |
| Someone's injured | Qualcuno è ferito
kwalkoonoh eh fereetoh |
| Someone's been knocked down | Qualcuno è stato investito
kwalkoonoh eh statoh eenvesteetoh |
| There's a fire at... | C'è un incendio a/in...
che oon eenchendyo ah/een |

YOU MAY HEAR...

Di quale servizio ha bisogno?
dee kwaleh serveetsyo ah beezonyo
Which service do you require?

Cos'è successo?
kozeh sootchessoh
What happened?

EMERGENCY SERVICES

l'idrante
leedranteh
hydrant

i vigili del fuoco
ee veejeelee del fwoko
firefighters

l'estintore
lesteentoreh
fire extinguisher

la volante
lah volanteh
police car

le manette
leh manetteh
handcuffs

l'allarme antincendio
lalarmeh anteenchendyo
fire alarm

il poliziotto
eel poleetsyottoh
policeman

l'ambulanza
lamboolantsa
ambulance

l'autopompa
lowtopompah
fire engine

POLICE AND CRIME

I want to report a crime	Desidero sporgere denuncia *deseederoh sporjereh denoonchya*
I've been...	Sono vittima... *sonoh veeteemah*
...robbed	...di un furto *dee oon foortoh*
...attacked	...di un attacco *dee oon attakko*
...mugged	...di un borseggio *dee oon borsedjoh*
...raped	...di una violenza sessuale *dee oonah vyolentsa sessooaleh*
...burgled	...di un furto *dee oon foortoh*
Someone has stolen...	Qualcuno ha rubato... *kwalkoonoh ah roobatoh*
...my car	...la mia auto *lah meeah owtoh*
...my money	...il mio denaro *eel meeoh denaroh*
...my passport	...il mio passaporto *eel meeah passaportoh*

YOU MAY HEAR...

Quando è successo?
kwandoh eh sootchessoh
When did it happen?

Si ricorda l'aspetto?
see reekordah laspettoh
What did he look like?

Ci sono
testimoni?
*chee sonoh
testeemonee*
**Was there a
witness?**

I'd like to speak to...	Vorrei parlare con... *vorray parlareh kon*
...a senior officer	...un responsabile *oon responsabeeleh*
...a policewoman	...una poliziotta *oonah poleetsyottah*
I need...	Ho bisogno di... *oh beezonyo dee*
...a lawyer	...un avvocato *oon avokatoh*
...an interpreter	...un interprete *oon eenterpreteh*
...to make a phone call	...fare una telefonata *fareh oonah telefonatah*
I'm very sorry, officer	Mi spiace molto, signor agente *mee spyacheh moltoh seenyor ajenteh*
Here is...	Ecco... *ekko*
...my driving licence	...la patente *lah patenteh*
...my insurance	...l'assicurazione *lasseekooratsyoneh*
How much is the fine?	A quanto ammonta la multa? *ah kwantoh ammontah lah mooltah*

YOU MAY HEAR...

Favorisca la patente per favore
favoreeska lah patenteh pehr favoreh
Your licence please

Favorisca i documenti
favoreeska ee dokomentee
Your papers

AT THE GARAGE

Where is the nearest garage?	Dov'è la più vicina autofficina? *doveh lah pew veecheenah owtoffeecheenah*
Can you do repairs?	Effettuate le riparazioni? *effettwateh leh reeparatsyonee*
I need...	Ho bisogno di... *oh beezonyo dee*
...a new tyre	...un nuovo pneumatico *oon nwovoh pneoomateekoh*
...a new exhaust	...un nuovo tubo di scarico *oon nwovoh tooboh dee skareekoh*
...a new windscreen	...un nuovo parabrezza *oon nwovoh parabretsa*
...a new bulb	...una nuova lampadina *oonah nwovah lampadeenah*
...wiper blades	...spazzole del tergicristallo *spatsoleh del terjeekreestalloh*
Do you have one in stock?	Ne avete in magazzino? *neh aveteh een magadzeenoh*
Can you replace this?	Può sostituirlo/a? *pwo sosteetweerloh/ah*
The...is not working	Il/la...non funziona *eel/lah...non foontsyonah*
There is something wrong with the engine	Il motore non funziona bene *eel motoreh non foontsyonah beneh*
Is it serious?	È grave? *eh graveh*
When will it be ready?	Quando sarà pronta? *kwandoh sarah prontah*
How much will it cost?	Quanto costerà? *kwantoh kosterah*

CAR BREAKDOWN

My car has broken down
La mia automobile è in panne
lah meeah owtomobeeleh eh een panneh

Please can you help me?
Mi può aiutare?
mee pwo ayewtareh

Please come to...
Venga a...
vengah ah

I have a puncture
Ho una gomma a terra
oh oonah gommah ah terrah

Can you help change the wheel?
Mi può aiutare a cambiare la ruota?
mee pwo ayewtareh ah kambyareh lah rwotah

I need a new tyre
Ho bisogno di un nuovo pneumatico
oh beezonyo dee oon nwovoh pneoomateekoh

My car won't start
La mia auto non si accende
lah meeah owtoh non see atchendeh

The engine is overheating
Il motore si sta surriscaldando
eel motoreh see stah sooreeskaldandoh

Can you fix it?
Può aggiustarla?
pwo adjoostarlah

YOU MAY HEAR...

Ha bisogno di aiuto?
ah beezonyo dee ayewtoh
Do you need any help?

Qual è il problema?
kwaleh eel problemah
What is the problem?

Ha la ruota di scorta?
ah lah rwotah dee skortah
Do you have a spare tyre?

LOST PROPERTY

I've lost...	Ho smarrito... *oh smareetoh*
...my money	...il mio denaro *eel meeoh denaroh*
...my keys	...le chiavi *leh kyavee*
...my glasses	...gli occhiali *lyee okyalee*
My luggage is missing	Il mio bagaglio è smarrito *eel meeoh bagalyo eh smareetoh*
My suitcase has been damaged	La mia valigia è stata danneggiata *la meeah valeeja eh statah dannedjatah*

il portafoglio
eel portafolyoh
wallet

il passaporto
eel passaportoh
passport

la carta di credito
lah kartah dee kredeetoh
credit card

il portamonete
eel portamoneteh
purse

la fotocamera
lah fotokamerah
camera

lo smartphone
loh smartphone
smartphone

la valigetta
lah valeejettah
briefcase

la borsa
lah borsah
handbag

la valigia
lah valeejah
suitcase

I need to phone my insurance company	Devo telefonare alla mia agenzia assicurativa *devoh telefonareh allah meeah ajentsya asseekoorateevah*
Can I put a stop on my credit cards?	Posso bloccare le mie carte di credito? *possoh blokareh leh mee- eh karteh dee kredeetoh*
My name is...	Mi chiamo... *mee kyamoh*
My policy number is...	Il numero della polizza è... *eel noomeroh dellah poleedza eh*
My address is...	Il mio indirizzo è... *eel meeo eendeereedzo eh*
My contact number is...	Il mio numero di telefono è... *eel meeoh noomeroh dee telefono eh*
My email address is...	Il mio indirizzo e-mail è... *eel meeoh eendeereedzo emayl eh*

MENU GUIDE

This guide lists the most common terms you may encounter on Italian menus or when shopping for food. If you can't find an exact phrase, try looking up its component parts.

A

abbacchio alla romana *Roman-style spring lamb*
acciughe sott'olio *anchovies in oil*
aceto *vinegar*
acqua *water*
acqua minerale gassata *sparkling mineral water*
acqua minerale non gassata *still mineral water*
acqua naturale *still mineral water, tap water*
affettato misto *variety of cold, sliced meats*
affogato al caffè *hot espresso on ice cream*
aglio *garlic*
agnello *lamb*
albicocche *apricots*
al forno *roast*
amatriciana *chopped bacon and tomato sauce*
ananas *pineapple*
anatra *duck*
anatra all'arancia *duck in orange sauce*
anguilla in umido *stewed eel*
anguria *watermelon*
antipasti *starters*
antipasti misti *mixed starters*
aperitivo *aperitif*
aragosta *lobster*

arancia *orange*
aranciata *orangeade; fresh orange juice*
aringa *herring*
arrosto *roast*
arrosto di tacchino *roast turkey*
asparagi *asparagus*
avocado all'agro *avocado with dressing*

B

baccalà *dried cod*
baccalà alla vicentina *Vicentine-style dried cod*
bagnacauda *vegetables (often raw) in a sauce of oil, garlic, and anchovy*
Barbaresco *dry red wine from Piedmont*
Barbera *dry red wine from Piedmont*
Bardolino *dry red wine from the Veneto region*
Barolo *dark, dry red wine from Piedmont*
basilico *basil*
bavarese *ice-cream cake; dessert made with cream*
Bel Paese *soft, white cheese*
besciamella *white sauce*
bignè *cream puff*
birra *beer*
birra chiara *light beer, lager*

birra grande *large beer*
birra piccola *small beer*
birra scura *dark beer*
bistecca ai ferri *grilled steak*
bistecca (di manzo) *steak*
bolognese *mince and tomato sauce*
braciola di maiale *pork steak*
branzino al forno *baked sea bass*
brasato *braised beef with herbs*
bresaola *dried, salted beef eaten with oil and lemon*
brioche *type of croissant*
brodo *clear broth*
brodo vegetale *clear vegetable broth*
bucatini *long tube pasta*
budino *pudding*
burro *butter*
burro di acciughe *anchovy butter*

C

Caciotta *tender, white cheese from Central Italy*
caffè *coffee*
caffè corretto *espresso with a dash of liqueur*
caffè latte *half coffee, half hot milk*
caffè lungo *weak espresso*
caffè macchiato *espresso with a dash of milk*
caffè ristretto *strong espresso*
calamari in umido *stewed squid*
calamaro *squid*
calzone *folded pizza with tomato and cheese*
camomilla *camomile tea*
cannella *cinnamon*
cannelloni al forno *baked pasta rolls filled with meat*

cappuccino *espresso with frothy milk sprinkled with cocoa powder*
capretto al forno *roast kid*
carbonara *sauce of egg, bacon, and cheese*
carciofi *artichokes*
carciofini sott'olio *baby artichokes in oil*
carne *meat*
carote *carrots*
carpaccio *finely sliced beef fillet with oil, lemon, and parmesan*
carré di maiale al forno *roast pork loin*
cassata siciliana *ice-cream cake with chocolate, glacé fruit, and ricotta*
castagne *chestnuts*
cavoletti di Bruxelles *Brussels sprouts*
cavolfiore *cauliflower*
cavolo *cabbage*
cefalo *grey mullet*
cernia *grouper (fish)*
cetriolo *cucumber*
charlotte *ice-cream cake with biscuits and fruit*
Chianti *dark red Tuscan wine*
cicoria *chicory*
cicorino *small chicory plants*
ciliege *cherries*
cime di rapa *sprouting broccoli*
cioccolata *chocolate*
cioccolata calda *hot chocolate*
cipolle *onions*
cocktail di gamberetti *shrimp cocktail*
conchiglie alla marchigiana *pasta shells in tomato sauce with ham, celery, carrot, and parsley*
coniglio *rabbit*

coniglio in umido *stewed rabbit*
consommé *clear broth*
contorni *vegetables*
coperto *cover charge*
coppa *cured neck of pork*
costata alla fiorentina *T-bone veal steak*
costata di manzo *T-bone beef steak*
cotechino *spiced pork sausage for boiling*
cotoletta *veal, pork, or lamb chop*
cotoletta ai ferri *grilled veal or pork chop*
cotoletta alla milanese *veal chop in breadcrumbs*
cotoletta alla valdostana *veal chop with ham and cheese, in breadcrumbs*
cotolette di agnello *lamb chops*
cotolette di maiale *pork chops*
cozze *mussels*
cozze alla marinara *mussels in white wine*
crema *custard dessert made with eggs and milk*
crema al caffè *coffee custard dessert*
crema al cioccolato *chocolate custard dessert*
crema di funghi *cream of mushroom soup*
crema di piselli *cream of pea soup*
crema pasticciera *confectioner's custard*
crêpes Suzette *pancakes flambéed with orange sauce*
crescente *fried bread made with flour, lard, and eggs*
crespelle *savoury pancakes*
crostata di frutta *fruit tart*

D, E

dadi *bouillon cubes*
datteri *dates*
degustazione di vini *wine tasting*
dentice al forno *baked dentex (type of sea bream)*
digestivo *digestive liqueur*
Dolcelatte *creamy blue cheese*
dolci *sweets, desserts, cakes*
endivia belga *white chicory*
entrecôte (di manzo) *beef entrecote*
espresso *strong, black coffee*

F

fagiano *pheasant*
fagioli *beans*
fagioli borlotti in umido *borlotti beans in tomatoes and vegetables*
fagiolini *long, green beans*
faraona *guinea fowl*
farcito *stuffed*
fegato *liver*
fegato alla veneta *liver in butter with onions*
fegato con salvia e burro *liver in butter and sage*
fettuccine *ribbon-shaped pasta*
fichi *figs*
filetti di pesce persico *fillets of perch*
filetti di sogliola *fillets of sole*
filetto ai ferri *grilled fillet of beef*
filetto al cognac *fillet of beef flambé*
filetto al pepe verde *fillet of beef with green peppercorns*
filetto al sangue *rare fillet of beef*
filetto ben cotto *well-done fillet of beef*
filetto (di manzo) *fillet of beef*

filetto medio *medium-cooked fillet of beef*
finocchi gratinati *fennel au gratin*
finocchio *fennel*
fonduta *cheese fondue*
formaggi misti *variety of cheeses*
fragole *strawberries*
fragole con gelato/panna *strawberries and ice cream/cream*
frappé *fruit or milk shake with crushed ice*
Frascati *dry white wine from area around Rome*
frittata *type of omelette*
frittata alle erbe *herb omelette*
fritto *deep fried*
fritto misto *mixed seafood in batter*
frittura di pesce *variety of fried fish*
frutta *fruit*
frutta alla fiamma *fruit flambé*
frutta secca *dried nuts and raisins*
frutti di bosco *mixture of strawberries, raspberries, mulberries, etc*
frutti di mare *seafood*
funghi *mushrooms*
funghi trifolati *mushrooms fried in garlic and parsley*

gamberetti *shrimps*
gamberi *prawns*
gamberoni *king prawns*
gazzosa *clear lemonade*
gelatina *jelly*
gelato *ice cream*
gelato di crema *vanilla-flavoured ice cream*

gelato di frutta *fruit-flavoured ice cream*
gnocchetti verdi agli spinaci e al gorgonzola *small flour, potato, and spinach dumplings with melted gorgonzola*
gnocchi *small flour and potato dumplings*
gnocchi alla romana *small milk and semolina dumplings with butter*
Gorgonzola *strong blue cheese from Lombardy*
grancevola *spiny spider crab*
granchio *crab*
granita *sorbet made of sweetened syrup*
grigliata di pesce *grilled fish*
grigliata mista *mixed grill (meat or fish)*
grissini *thin, crisp breadsticks*
Gruviera *Gruyère cheese*

I

indivia *endive*
insalata *salad*
insalata caprese *salad of tomatoes and mozzarella*
insalata di funghi porcini *boletus mushroom salad*
insalata di mare *seafood salad*
insalata di nervetti *boiled beef or veal tendons served cold with beans and pickles*
insalata di pomodori *tomato salad*
insalata di riso *rice salad*
insalata mista *mixed salad*
insalata russa *Russian salad*
insalata verde *green salad*
involtini *meat rolls stuffed with ham and herbs*

L

lamponi *raspberries*
lasagne al forno *layers of pasta baked in meat sauce with cheese*
latte *milk*
latte macchiato con cioccolato *hot milk sprinkled with cocoa*
lattuga *lettuce*
leggero *light*
legumi *legumes or pulses*
lemonsoda *sparkling lemon drink*
lenticchie *lentils*
lepre *hare*
limonata *lemon-flavoured fizzy drink*
limone *lemon*
lingua *tongue*

M

macedonia di frutta *fruit salad*
maiale *pork*
maionese *mayonnaise*
mandarino *mandarin*
mandorla *almond*
manzo *beef*
marroni *large chestnuts*
Marsala *fortified wine*
marzapane *marzipan*
Mascarpone *soft, mild cheese*
medaglioni di vitello *veal medallions*
mela *apple*
melagrana *pomegranate*
melanzane *aubergine*
melone *melon*
menta *mint*
meringata *meringue pie*
merluzzo *cod*
merluzzo alla pizzaiola *cod in tomato sauce with anchovies and capers*
merluzzo in bianco *cod with oil and lemon*

messicani in gelatina *rolls of veal in jelly*
millefoglie *pastry layered with custard*
minestra in brodo *noodle soup*
minestrone *vegetable soup with rice or pasta*
mirtilli *bilberries*
more *mulberries or blackberries*
moscato *sweet wine*
mousse al cioccolato *chocolate mousse*
Mozzarella *soft cheese*
mozzarella in carrozza *fried slices of bread and mozzarella*

N, O

nasello *hake*
nocciole *hazelnuts*
noce moscata *nutmeg*
noci *walnuts*
nodino *veal chop*
olio *oil*
origano *oregano*
ossobuco *stewed shin of veal*
ostriche *oysters*

P

paglia e fieno *mixed plain and green tagliatelle*
paillard di manzo *slices of grilled beef*
paillard di vitello *slices of grilled veal*
pane *bread*
panino *filled roll; bread roll*
panna *cream*
parmigiana di melanzane *aubergines baked with cheese*
pasta al forno *pasta baked in white sauce and grated cheese*
pasta e fagioli *thick soup with borlotti beans and pasta rings*

pasta e piselli *pasta with peas*
pasticcio di fegato d'oca *baked pasta dish with goose liver*
pasticcio di lepre *baked pasta dish with hare*
pasticcio di maccheroni *baked macaroni*
pastina in brodo *soup with small pasta*
patate *potatoes*
patate al forno/arrosto *roast potatoes*
patate fritte *chips*
patate in insalata *potato salad*
Pecorino *strong, hard cheese made from sheep's milk*
penne *pasta quills*
penne ai quattro formaggi *pasta with four cheeses sauce*
penne all'arrabbiata *pasta with tomato and chilli pepper sauce*
penne panna e prosciutto *pasta with cream and ham sauce*
pepe *pepper (spice)*
peperoncino *crushed chilli pepper*
peperoni *peppers*
peperoni ripieni *stuffed peppers*
peperoni sott'olio *peppers in oil*
pera *pear*
pesca *peach*
pesce *fish*
pesce al cartoccio *fish baked in foil with herbs*
pesce in carpione *marinaded fish*
pesto *sauce of basil, pine nuts, Parmesan, garlic, and oil*
Pinot *dry white wine from the Veneto region*
pinzimonio *sauce with oil and vinegar served with raw vegetables*

piselli *peas*
piselli al prosciutto *peas with ham and basil*
pizzaiola *slices of cooked beef in tomato sauce, oregano, and anchovies*
pizzoccheri alla Valtellinese *pasta strips with vegetables and cheese*
polenta *boiled cornmeal left to set and sliced*
polenta e osei *polenta with small birds*
polenta pasticciata *layers of polenta, tomato sauce, and cheese*
pollo *chicken*
pollo alla cacciatora *chicken in white wine with onions and carrots*
pollo alla diavola *deep-fried chicken pieces*
polpette *meatballs*
polpettone *meatloaf*
pomodori *tomatoes*
pomodori ripieni *stuffed tomatoes*
pompelmo *grapefruit*
porri *leeks*
prezzemolo *parsley*
primi piatti *first courses*
prosciutto cotto *cooked ham*
prosciutto crudo *type of cured ham*
prugne *plums*
punte di asparagi all'agro *asparagus tips in oil and lemon*
purè di patate *mashed potatoes*
puttanesca *tomato sauce with anchovies, capers, and black olives*

Q, R

quaglie *quails*
radicchio *red chicory*
ragù *meat-based sauce*
rapanelli *radishes*
ravioli *stuffed pasta parcels*
ravioli al pomodoro *meat ravioli in tomato sauce*
razza *skate*
Ricotta *type of cottage cheese*
risi e bisi *risotto with peas and ham*
riso *rice*
risotto *rice cooked in stock*
risotto alla castellana *risotto with mushroom, ham, cream, and cheese*
risotto alla milanese *risotto with saffron*
risotto al nero di seppia *risotto with cuttlefish ink*
risotto al tartufo *truffle risotto*
roast-beef all'inglese *thinly sliced cold roast beef*
Robiola *type of soft cheese from Lombardy*
rognone trifolato *kidney in garlic, oil, and parsley*
rosatello/rosato *rosé wine*
rosmarino *rosemary*

S

salame *salami*
sale *salt*
salmone affumicato *smoked salmon*
salsa cocktail/rosa *mayonnaise and ketchup sauce for fish and seafood*
salsa di pomodoro *tomato sauce*

salsa tartara *tartar sauce*
salsa vellutata *white sauce made with clear broth*
salsa verde *sauce for meat, with parsley and oil*
salsiccia *sausage*
salsiccia di cinghiale *wild boar sausage*
salsiccia di maiale *pork sausage*
saltimbocca alla romana *slices of veal stuffed with ham and sage and fried*
salvia *sage*
sambuca (con la mosca) *aniseed-flavour liqueur served with a coffee bean*
sarde ai ferri *grilled sardines*
scaloppine *veal escalopes*
scaloppine al prezzemolo *veal escalopes with parsley*
scamorza alla griglia *grilled soft cheese*
scampi alla griglia *grilled scampi*
secco *dry*
secondi piatti *second courses, main courses*
sedano *celery*
selvaggina *game*
semifreddo *cake or dessert often containing cream and served chilled*
senape *mustard*
seppie in umido *stewed cuttlefish*
servizio compreso *service charge included*
servizio escluso *service charge excluded*
Soave *dry white wine from the Veneto region*
sogliola *sole*
sogliola ai ferri *grilled sole*

sogliola al burro *sole cooked in butter*

sogliola alla mugnaia *sole cooked in flour and butter*

sorbetto *sorbet, soft ice cream*

soufflé al formaggio *cheese soufflé*

soufflé al prosciutto *ham soufflé*

speck *cured, smoked ham*

spezzatino di vitello *veal stew*

spiedini *assorted chunks of spit-cooked meat or fish*

spinaci *spinach*

spinaci all'agro *spinach with oil and lemon*

spremuta di... *freshly squeezed...juice*

spumante *sparkling wine*

Stracchino *soft cheese from Lombardy*

stracciatella *soup of beaten eggs in clear broth*

strudel di mele *apple strudel*

stufato *braised*

succo di... *...juice*

sugo al tonno *tomato sauce with tuna, garlic, and parsley*

T

tacchino ripieno *stuffed turkey*

tagliata *finely cut beef fillet cooked in the oven*

tagliatelle *thin ribbon-shaped pasta*

tagliatelle rosse *tagliatelle made with beetroot*

tagliatelle verdi *tagliatelle made with spinach*

tagliolini *thin soup noodles*

tartine *small sandwiches*

tartufo *ice cream covered in cocoa or chocolate; truffle*

tè *tea*

tiramisù *dessert with coffee-soaked sponge, Marsala, Mascarpone, and cocoa powder*

tonno *tuna*

torta *tart, flan*

torta di ricotta *type of cheesecake*

torta salata *savoury flan*

tortellini *pasta shapes filled with minced pork, ham, Parmesan, and nutmeg*

trancio di palombo *smooth dogfish steak*

trancio di pesce spada *swordfish steak*

trenette col pesto *flat spaghetti with pesto sauce*

triglia *mullet (fish)*

trippa *tripe*

trota *trout*

trota affumicata *smoked trout*

trota al burro *trout cooked in butter*

trota alle mandorle *trout with almonds*

trota bollita *boiled trout*

U

uccelletti *small birds wrapped in bacon, served on cocktail sticks*

uova *eggs*

uova alla coque *soft-boiled eggs*

uova al tegamino con pancetta *fried eggs and bacon*

uova farcite *eggs with tuna, capers, and mayonnaise filling*

uova sode *hard-boiled eggs*

uva *grapes*

uva bianca *white grapes*

uva nera *black grapes*

V

vellutata di asparagi
*creamed asparagus with
egg yolks*
vellutata di piselli
*creamed peas with
egg yolks*
verdura *vegetables*
vermicelli *long,
very fine, thin pasta*
vino *wine*
vino bianco
white wine
vino da dessert
dessert wine
vino da pasto *table wine*
vino da tavola *table wine*
vino rosso *red wine*
vitello *veal*
vitello tonnato *cold sliced
veal in tuna, anchovy, oil,
and lemon sauce*
vongole *clams*

W, Z

würstel *hot dog*
zabaglione *creamy dessert
of eggs, sugar, and Marsala*
zafferano *saffron*
zucca *pumpkin*
zucchero *sugar*
zucchine *courgettes*
zucchine al pomodoro
*courgettes in tomato, garlic
and parsley sauce*
zucchine ripiene
stuffed courgettes
zuccotto *ice-cream cake
with sponge fingers, cream,
and chocolate*
zuppa *soup*
zuppa di cipolle *onion soup*
zuppa di cozze *mussel soup*
zuppa di lenticchie *lentil soup*
zuppa di pesce *fish soup*
zuppa di verdura *vegetable soup*
zuppa inglese *trifle*

The gender of an Italian noun is shown by the word for "the": il or lo (masculine), la (feminine), and their plural forms i or gli (masculine) and le (feminine). When lo or la are abbreviated to l' in front of a vowel or h, the gender of the noun is shown by the abbreviation (m) or (f) after it.

A

a little *un poco*
a lot *molto*
about *circa*
above *sopra*
accident *l'incidente (m)*
accident and emergency
   il Pronto Soccorso
accommodation *alloggio*
account number
   il numero di conto
across *attraverso*
activities *le attività (f)*
actor *l'attore (m)*
actress *l'attrice (f)*
adapter *l'adattatore (m)*
add (verb) *sommare*
address *l'indirizzo (m)*
adhesive tape *lo scotch*
adult *l'adulto (m)*
aerobics *l'aerobica (f)*
aeroplane *l'aeroplano (m)*
after *dopo*
afternoon *il pomeriggio*
aftersun *il doposole (m)*
again *ancora*
air conditioning
   l'aria condizionata (f)
air stewardess
   l'assistente di volo (f)
aircraft *l'aeroplano (m)*
airmail *la posta aerea*
airport *l'aeroporto (m)*

aisle *la corsia (f)*
aisle seat *il posto*
   vicino al corridoio
alarm clock *la sveglia (f)*
alcoholic drinks
   le bevande alcoliche (f)
all *tutto*
allergic *allergico/a*
allergy *l'allergia (f)*
almost *quasi*
alone *solo/a*
along *lungo*
already *già*
altitude *la quota*
always *sempre*
ambulance
   l'ambulanza (f)
amount *l'importo (m)*
and *e*
angry *arrabbiato/a*
animals *gli animali*
ankle *la caviglia*
anorak *il giaccone (m)*
another *altro/a*
answering machine
   la segreteria telefonica
answer (verb) *rispondere*
antibiotics *gli antibiotici*
antiseptic *il disinfettante (m)*
anything *niente; qualcosa*
apartment block
   il condominio (m)
appearance *l'aspetto (m)*

applaud (verb) *applaudire*
apple *la mela (f)*
apple juice
il succo di mela (m)
application *l'applicazione (f)*
appointment
l'appuntamento (m)
apricot *l'albicocca (f)*
April *aprile*
apron *il grembiule*
arc *l'arco (m)*
arch *l'arco plantare (m)*
architect *l'architetto (m)*
architecture
l'architettura (f)
area *la superficie (f)*
arm *il braccio*
armband *il bracciolo*
around *attorno*
arrangements
gli accordi
arrivals hall *gli arrivi*
arrive (verb) *arrivare*
art *l'arte (f)*
art gallery *la galleria d'arte*
arthritis *l'artrite (f)*
artificial sweetener
il dolcificante
artist *l'artista (f)*
as *come*
ashtray *il posacenere (m)*
assistant *l'assistente (m/f)*
asthma *l'asma (f)*
at *a*
athlete *l'atleta (m)*
ATM *il bancomat (m)*
attachment *l'allegato (m)*
attack *l'attacco (m)*
attend (verb) *partecipare*
attractions
i luoghi d'interesse (m)
aubergine *la melanzana (f)*
audience *il pubblico (m)*

audio guide *l'audio guida*
August *agosto*
aunt *la zia (f)*
Australia *Australia (f)*
automatic *automatico*
automatic ticket machine
la biglietteria automatica
autumn *l'autunno (m)*
avenue *il viale (m)*
avocado *l'avocado (m)*
awful *orribile*

B

baby *il bimbo (m)*
baby changing facilities
lo spazio con fasciatoio (m)
babysitting
il servizio di babysitting
back (body) *la schiena*
back (not front of) *la parte
posteriore*
backpack *lo zaino*
bacon *la pancetta (f)*
bad *cattivo/a*
badminton *il volano*
bag *la borsa*
bagel *il bagel*
baggage allowance
il bagaglio consentito
baggage reclaim
il ritiro bagagli
baguette *il filone*
baker's *la panetteria*
bakery *il panificio*
bake (verb) *cuocere al forno*
baking tray *la teglia da forno*
balcony *il balcone*
ball *la palla*
ballet *la danza*
banana *la banana*
bandage *la benda*
bank *la banca*
bank account *il conto bancario*

bank charge
  la commissione bancaria
bank holiday *il giorno festivo*
bank manager
  il direttore della banca
bank transfer *il bonifico*
bar *il bar*
barbecue
  la griglia per barbecue
barber *il barbiere*
bar snacks *gli stuzzichini*
bartender *il barista*
baseball mitt
  il guanto da baseball
basement *il seminterrato*
basil *il basilico*
basket *il cestino*
basketball *la palla da basket*
bath *il bagno*
bath robe *l'accappatoio (m)*
bathroom *il bagno*
bath towel
  l'asciugamano grande (m)
bathtub *la vasca*
battery *la batteria*
beach *la spiaggia*
beach ball
  il pallone da spiaggia
beach towel
  il telo da spiaggia
beans *i chicchi*
bear *l'orso (m)*
beautiful *bello/a*
bed *il letto*
bed and breakfast
  la pensione con colazione
bed linen *la biancheria da letto*
bedroom *la camera da letto*
bee *l'ape (f)*
beef *il manzo*
beer *la birra*
beetle *il coleottero*
beetroot *la barbabietola*

before *prima di*
beginner
  principiante (m/f)
beginning *l'inizio*
behind *dietro a*
bell *il campanello*
below *sotto*
belt *la cintura*
bench *la panca*
beneath *sotto*
berry *la bacca*
beside *vicino a*
better *migliore*
between *tra*
be (verb) *essere*
beyond *oltre*
bicycle *la bicicletta*
big *grande*
bike rack *il cavalletto*
bikini *il bikini*
bill *il conto*
birds *gli uccelli*
birth *la nascita*
birth certificate
  il certificato di nascita
birthday *il compleanno*
biscuit *il biscotto*
bite *il morso*
bitter *amaro*
black *nero/a*
black coffee *il caffè nero*
black tea *il tè nero*
blackberry *la mora*
blackcurrant *il ribes nero*
blanket *la coperta*
bleach *la candeggina*
blender *il frullatore*
blister *la vescica*
block *la parata*
block of flats *il condominio*
blonde *biondo*
blood pressure
  la pressione sanguigna

blood test *le analisi del sangue*
blouse *la camicetta*
blow dry (verb)
  asciugare con il fon
blue *blu*
blueberry *il mirtillo*
blusher *il fard*
board (verb) *imbarcarsi*
boarding gate
  l'uscita d'imbarco (f)
boarding pass
  la carta d'imbarco
boat *la barca*
body *il corpo*
body lotion
  la crema per il corpo
boil (verb) *bollire*
bonnet (car) *il cofano*
book *il libro*
book (verb) *prenotare*
book a flight (verb)
  prenotare un volo
book shop *la libreria*
boot *lo stivale*
boot (car) *il bagagliaio*
bored *annoiato*
borrow (verb) *prendere
  in prestito*
bottle *la bottiglia*
bottle opener
  l'apribottiglie (m)
bottled water *l'acqua in
  bottiglia (f)*
boutique *la boutique*
bowl *la scodella*
bowling *il bowling*
box *la scatola*
box office *la biglietteria*
boy *il ragazzo*
boyfriend *il fidanzato*
bracelet *il bracciale*
brain *il cervello*
brake *il freno*

branch *il ramo*
bread *il pane*
breakdown *il guasto*
breakfast *la colazione*
breakfast buffet
  il buffet della colazione
breakfast cereals
  i cereali da colazione
brick *il mattone*
bridge *il dorso
  del piede*
briefcase *la valigetta*
briefs *lo slip*
brioche *la brioche*
British *britannico/a*
broccoli *il broccolo*
broken *rotto/a*
broom *la scopa*
brother *il fratello*
brown *marrone*
brown bread *il pane integrale*
brown rice *il riso integrale*
browse (verb) *navigare*
bruise *l'ematoma (m)*
brunette *bruno*
brush *la spazzola*
brush (cleaning) *la scopa*
bubblebath *il bagnoschiuma*
bucket *il secchio*
buckle *la fibbia*
buffet *il buffet*
build (verb) *costruire*
builder *il muratore*
building site *il cantiere*
bulb *il bulbo*
bumper *il paraurti*
bun *la pastina*
bunch *il mazzetto*
buoy *la boa*
bureau de change
  l'ufficio di cambio (m)
burger *l'hamburger (m)*
burgle (verb) *svaligiare*

burn *la bruciatura*
bus *l'autobus (m)*
bus driver *l'autista*
bus station *la stazione
   degli autobus*
bus stop *la fermata
   dell'autobus*
bus ticket *il biglietto*
business, on *per lavoro*
bust *il busto*
butcher's *la macelleria*
butter *il burro*
butternut squash
   la zucca Butternut
button *il bottone*
buy (verb) *comprare*
by *da; vicino a*

C

cab *taxi*
cabin *la cabina*
cable *il cavo*
cable car *la funivia*
cable television
   la televisione via cavo
café *il bar*
cafetière *la caffettiera*
cakes *i dolci*
calculator *la calcolatrice*
calendar *il calendario*
call button *il pulsante
   di chiamata*
calm *calmo/a*
camera *la fotocamera*
camera bag *la borsa
   per fotocamera*
camera case *la custodia*
camisole *il corpetto*
camp (verb) *campeggiare*
camping kettle *il bollitore*
camping stove *il fornetto
   da campeggio*
campsite *il campeggio*

Canada *il Canada*
can (noun) *la scatoletta*
can (verb) *potere*
canoe *la canoa*
can opener *l'apribottiglie (m)*
cap *la cuffia*
capital *la capitale*
cappuccino *il cappuccino*
capsule *la capsula*
car *la macchina*
car accident
   l'incidente stradale
caravan *il camper*
card *il biglietto d'auguri*
cardboard *il cartone*
cardigan *il cardigan*
cards *le carte*
car hire *l'autonoleggio (m)*
car park *il parcheggio*
car rental desk *l'ufficio
   dell'autonoleggio (m)*
car wash *l'autolavaggio*
carnival *il carnevale*
carpet *il tappeto*
carrot *la carota*
carry (verb) *portare*
carton *il cartone*
case *la custodia*
cash *il denaro*
cash machine
   il sportello bancomat
cashier *il cassiere*
cash (verb) *riscuotere*
casino *il casinò*
casserole dish *la casseruola*
castle *il castello*
casual *casual*
cat *il gatto*
catamaran *il catamarano*
catch (verb) *prendere*
cathedral *la cattedrale*
cauliflower *il cavolfiore*
caution *attenzione*

cave *la caverna*
CD *il CD*
ceiling *il soffitto*
celebration *la festa*
central heating
   il riscaldamento centralizzato
centre *il centro*
cereal *il cereale*
chair *la sedia*
chair lift *la seggiovia*
champagne *lo champagne*
change (verb) *cambiare*
changing room *il spogliatoio*
changing rooms *i camerini*
channel *il canale*
channel (TV) *il canale*
charge *l'imputazione (f)*
charge (verb) *addebitare*
chart *la scheda del paziente*
check in *il check-in*
check in (verb) *fare il check-in*
check-in desk *il banco*
   accettazione
check out (hotel) *lasciare*
check-out (supermarket)
   la cassa
checkup *il controllo*
cheek *la guancia*
cheers! *cin cin!*
cheese *il formaggio*
chef *il cuoco*
chemist *la farmacia*
cheque *l'assegno (m)*
cheque card *la carta assegni*
chequebook *il libretto*
   degli assegni
cherry *la ciliegia*
cherry tomato
   il pomodoro ciliegino
chest *il torace*
chewing gum
   la gomma da masticare
chicken *il pollo*

chickpeas *i ceci*
child *bambino/a (m/f)*
children *i bambini*
chill *l'infreddatura (f)*
chilli *il peperoncino*
chin *il mento*
chocolate *il cioccolatino*
choke (verb) *soffocare*
chop *la costoletta*
chorizo *il chorizo*
church *la chiesa*
cigar *il sigaro*
cigarette *la sigaretta*
cigarettes *le sigarette*
cinema *il cinema*
cinnamon *la cannella*
circle *il cerchio*
citrus fruit *gli agrumi*
city *la città*
clam *la vongola*
clean *pulito/a*
client *il cliente*
cliff *la scogliera*
clinic *la clinica*
clock *l'orologio*
clock radio *la radiosveglia*
close (near) *vicino*
close (verb) *chiudere*
closed *chiuso/a*
clothes *gli abiti*
clothing *l'abbigliamento (m)*
cloud *la nuvola*
cloudy *nuvoloso/a*
club *il fiore*
clubbing *andare in discoteca*
coach *il pullman*
coast *la costa*
coaster *il sottobicchiere*
coastguard *il guardacoste*
coat *il cappotto*
coat hanger
   l'appendiabiti (m)
cockroach *la blatta*

cocktail *il cocktail*
coconut *la noce di cocco*
cod *il merluzzo*
coffee *il caffè*
coffee cup *la tazzina da caffè*
coffee machine
  la macchina del caffè
coffee table *il tavolino*
coin *la moneta*
colander *il colino*
cold *freddo/a*
cold (illness) *il raffreddore*
collection *la collezione*
college *l'università*
colouring pencil
  la matita colorata
colours *i colori*
comb *il pettine*
come (verb) *venire*
comic *il fumetto*
company *la ditta*
compartment *il scompartimento*
compass *la bussola*
complain (verb) *reclamare*
complaint *la denuncia*
computer *il computer*
concert *il concerto*
concourse *l'atrio (m)*
conditioner *il balsamo*
condom *il preservativo*
confident *sicuro/a di sé*
confused *confuso/a*
connection *la coincidenza*
constipation *la stitichezza*
consul *il console*
consulate *il consolato*
consultation *la visita*
contact lenses
  le lenti a contatto
contact number
  il numero di telefono
container *il contenitore*
contents *il contenuto*

continent *continente*
contraception
  la contraccezione
cooking *cucinare*
coolbox *il frigo portatile*
copy (verb) *copiare*
coral reef *la barriera corallina*
core *il torsolo*
coriander *il coriandolo*
cork *il tappo*
corkscrew *il cavatappi*
corn *il mais*
corner *il calcio d'angolo*
correct *vero/a*
cot *il lettino*
cotton *il cotone*
couchette *la cuccetta*
cough *la tosse*
cough medicine
  la medicina per la tosse
counter *la pedina*
country *il Paese*
count (verb) *contare*
couple *la coppia*
courgette *la zucchina*
courier *il corriere*
course *il piatto*
courses *le portate*
courtyard *il cortile*
cousin *il cugino*
cow *la mucca*
crab *il granchio*
cramp *il crampo*
cream (lotion) *la crema*
cream cheese
  il formaggio cremoso
crease *la linea*
credit card *la carta di credito*
crêpes *le crêpes*
crime *il reato*
crisps *le patatine*
croissant *il cornetto*
cross trainer *l'ellittica (f)*

crushed *tritato/a*
crust *la crosta*
cry (verb) *piangere*
cucumber *il cetriolo*
cufflinks *i gemelli*
cup *la tazza*
curly *riccio*
current account
  il conto corrente
curry *il curry*
curtain *il sipario*
cushion *il cuscino*
customer *il cliente*
customs *la dogana*
cut *il taglio*
cutlery *le posate*
cycle lane *la pista ciclabile*
cycle (verb) *andare in bici*
cycling helmet *il casco*

D

dairy *i latticini*
damaged *danneggiato/a*
dance *la musica da ballo*
dancing *ballare*
danger *pericolo*
dark *scuro/a*
dashboard *il cruscotto*
daughter *la figlia*
day *il giorno*
debit card *la carta di debito*
December *dicembre*
deck chair *la sedia a sdraio*
deep-fried *fritto*
  in olio abbondante
degrees *gradi*
delayed *ritardato/a*
delicatessen *la gastronomia*
delicious *delizioso/a*
delivery *il parto*
dentist *il/la dentista*
deodorant *il deodorante*
department *il dipartimento*

department store
  il grande magazzino
departure board
  il tabellone delle partenze
departure lounge
  la sala delle partenze
departures *le partenze*
departures hall
  le partenze
deposit *il deposito*
desert *il deserto*
desk *la scrivania*
dessert *il dessert*
destination *la destinazione*
detergent *il detergente*
develop (film) *sviluppare*
diabetic *diabetico/a*
dial (verb) *comporre*
diarrhoea *la diarrea*
diary *l'agenda (f)*
dictionary *il dizionario*
diesel *il diesel*
difficult *difficile*
digital camera
  la fotocamera digitale
digital radio *la radio digitale*
dining car *la carrozza ristorante*
dining room *la sala da pranzo*
dinner *la cena*
direct debit
  l'addebito diretto (m)
directions *Indicazioni*
dirty *sporco*
disabled parking
  il parcheggio per disabili
discuss (verb) *discutere*
disembark (verb)
  sbarcare
dish *il piatto*
dishwasher *la lavastoviglie*
distance *la distanza*
district *il distretto*
dive (verb) *tuffarsi*

divorced *divorziato/a*
doctor *il dottore*
doctor's surgery
  l'ambulatorio (m)
dog *il cane*
doll *la bambola*
dolphin *il delfino*
don't *non*
door *la porta*
doorbell *il campanello*
dosage *il dosaggio*
double bed *il letto
  matrimoniale*
double room
  la camera doppia
do (verb) *fare*
down *giù*
download (verb) *scaricare*
drain *il canale di scolo*
drawer *il cassetto*
drawing *il disegno*
draw (verb) *disegnare*
dress *l'abito (m)*
dressing *la fasciatura*
drink (noun) *la bibita*
drink (verb) *bere*
drinks *le bibite*
drive (verb) *guidare*
driver *l'autista (m)*
driving licence
  la patente di guida
dry (day; clothes) *asciutto/a*
dry (wine) *secco*
duck *l'anatra (f)*
during *durante*
dust pan *la paletta*
dustbin *la pattumiera*
duty-free shop *il negozio
  duty-free*
duvet *il piumone*
DVD *il disco DVD*
DVD player
  il lettore DVD

E

each *ciascuno*
each (every) *ogni*
ear *l'orecchio (m)*
early *presto*
earrings *l'orecchino (m)*
earthquake *il terremoto*
east *l'est (m)*
easy *facile*
eat-in *mangiare sul posto*
eating out *mangiare fuori*
eat (verb) *mangiare*
egg *l'uovo (m)*
eight *otto*
elbow *il gomito*
electric razor *il rasoio elettrico*
electrician *l'elettricista (m)*
electricity *l'elettricità (f)*
eleven *undici*
email *l'e-mail (f)*
email address
  l'indirizzo e-mail (m)
embarrassed *imbarazzata*
embassy *l'ambasciata (f)*
emergency *l'emergenza (f)*
emergency exit *l'uscita di
  emergenza (f)*
emergency room
  il pronto soccorso
emergency services
  gli servizi di emergenza
emigrate (verb) *emigrare*
empty *vuoto/a*
end *la fine*
engaged/busy *occupato/a*
engine *il motore*
English *inglese*
engraving *l'incisione (f)*
enjoy (verb) *divertirsi*
entrance *l'entrata (f)*
entrance ticket
  il biglietto d'entrata
envelope *la busta*

epileptic *epilettico/a*
equipment *l'attrezzatura (f)*
espresso *l'espresso (m)*
estate agent's *l'agenzia immobiliare (f)*
euro *l'euro (m)*
evening *la sera*
evening dress *l'abito da sera (m)*
evening menu *il menù della cena*
events *le discipline*
every *tutti*
exactly *esattamente*
examine (verb) *esaminare*
exchange rate *il tasso di cambio*
excited *entusiasta*
excursion *l'escursione (f)*
excuse me *mi scusi*
exercise bike *la bicicletta*
exhaust (car) *la marmitta*
exhibition *l'esposizione (f)*
exit *l'uscita (f)*
expensive *caro/a*
expiry date *la data di scadenza*
express service *il servizio espresso*
extension lead *la prolunga*
extra *extra*
eye *l'occhio (m)*
eyebrow *il sopracciglio*
eyelash *il ciglio*
eyeliner *la matita per gli occhi*

F

fabric *il tessuto*
face *il viso*
faint (verb) *svenire*
fairground *il luna park*
family *la famiglia*
family room *la camera familiare*
family ticket *il biglietto famiglia*
fan *il ventilatore*
far *lontano*
fare *la tariffa*

farm *la fattoria*
farmer *l'agricoltore (m)*
fashion *la moda*
fast *veloce*
fast food *il fast food*
fat *il grasso*
father *il padre*
favourite *preferito/a*
February *febbraio*
female *la donna*
fence *il recinto*
ferry *il traghetto*
festivals *le feste*
fever *la febbre*
field *il campo*
fifty *cinquanta*
fillet *il filetto*
film *la pellicola*
film (camera) *il rullino*
find (verb) *trovare*
fine (legal) *la multa*
finger *il dito*
finish (verb) *finire*
fire *l'incendio (m)*
fire alarm *l'allarme antincendio (m)*
fire engine *l'autopompa (f)*
fire escape *la scala di sicurezza*
fire extinguisher *l'estintore (m)*
firefighter *il pompiere*
first *primo/a*
first aid *il pronto soccorso*
first-aid box *la cassetta di pronto soccorso*
first floor *il primo piano*
fish *il pesce*
fishing rod *la canna da pesca*
fishmonger *il pescivendolo*
fitness *il fitness*
five *cinque*
fix (verb) *riparare*
flag *la bandierina*
flash gun *il flash*

flash photography *la fotografia con il flash*
flat *il bemolle*
flight *il volo*
flight attendant *l'assistente di volo (f)*
flight meal *il pasto a bordo*
flight number *il numero del volo*
flip-flop *l'infradito (f)*
flippers *le pinne*
float *la tavoletta*
flood *l'inondazione (f)*
floor *il pavimento*
florist *la fioraia/il fioraio*
flowers *i fiori*
flu *l'influenza (f)*
fly (verb) *volare*
fog *la nebbia*
food *il cibo*
foot *il piede*
football (ball) *il pallone*
football (game) *il calcio*
footpath *il sentiero*
for *per*
foreign currency *la valuta estera*
forest *la foresta*
fork *la forchetta*
fortnight *quindici giorni*
forty *quaranta*
forward *l'attaccante (m)*
fountain *la fontana*
four *quattro*
fracture *la frattura*
fragile *fragile*
frame *la struttura*
free *libero*
free (no charge) *gratis*
free (not occupied) *libero/a*
freeze *la gelata*
fresh *fresco/a*
Friday *venerdì*
fridge-freezer *il frigorifero congelatore*

fried *fritto*
friend *l'amico/a (m/f)*
from *da*
front; in front of *davanti; di fronte a*
front door *il portone*
frost *il gelo*
frozen *congelato/a*
fruit *la frutta*
frying pan *la padella*
fry (verb) *friggere*
fuel gauge *l'indicatore di livello del carburante (m)*
full *pieno/a*
furniture shop *il negozio di arredamento*
fuse box *la scatola dei fusibili*

G

gallery (theatre) *la galleria*
game *il gioco*
garage *il garage*
garden *il giardino*
garlic *l'aglio (m)*
gas *il gas*
gate *il cancello*
gear stick *la leva del cambio*
get off (verb) *scendere*
gift *il regalo*
gift shop *il negozio di articoli da regalo*
gin *il gin*
ginger *lo zenzero*
giraffe *la giraffa*
girl *la ragazza*
girlfriend *la fidanzata*
give (verb) *dare*
glass *il vetro*
glass (drinking) *il bicchiere*
glasses *gli occhiali*
gloss *lucido/a*
gloves *i guanti*
glue *la colla*

go (verb) *andare*
go out (verb) *uscire*
goggles *gli occhialini*
gold *l'oro (m)*
golf *il golf*
golf ball *la palla da golf*
golf club *la mazza*
golf course *il campo da golf*
golf tee *il tee*
good *buono/a*
good afternoon *buon pomeriggio*
good evening *buonasera*
good morning *buongiorno*
good night *buonanotte*
goodbye *arrivederci*
gram *il grammo*
grater *la grattugia*
graze *l'escoriazione (f)*
Great Britain *la Gran Bretagna*
green *verde*
green tea *il tè verde*
greengrocer *il fruttivendolo*
grey *grigio/a*
grill (verb) *cuocere alla griglia*
grill pan *la griglia*
groceries *la spesa*
ground *macinato*
group *il gruppo*
guarantee *la garanzia*
guest *l'ospite (m/f)*
guide (person) *la guida*
guidebook *la guida*
guided tour *la visita guidata*
gym *la palestra*

H

hail *la grandine*
hair *i capelli*
hairdresser's *il parrucchiere*
hairdryer *l'asciugacapelli (m)*
half *la metà; mezzo/a (adj)*
hand *la mano*

hand luggage
  il bagaglio a mano
handbag *la borsa*
handle *la maniglia*
happen (verb) *succedere*
happy *contento/a; felice*
harbour *il porto*
hard *duro/a*
hardware shop *la ferramenta*
hat *il cappello*
hatchback *il portellone*
hate (verb) *odiare*
have (verb) *avere*
hayfever *il raffreddore da fieno*
hazard lights *le frecce lampeggianti*
he *egli; lui*
head *la testa*
head rest *il poggiatesta*
headache *il mal di testa*
headlight *i fari*
headphones *le cuffie*
health *la salute*
health insurance
  l'assicurazione sanitaria
hear (verb) *sentire*
heart *il cuore*
heart condition
  la patologia cardiaca
heater *l'impianto di riscaldamento (m)*
heating
  il riscaldamento
heavy *pesante*
heel *il tallone*
height *l'altezza*
hello *ciao; buongiorno*
hello (on phone) *pronto*
help *aiuto*
help (verb) *aiutare*
her (object) *lei; le*
her (possessive) *suo/sua (sing)/sue/suoi (plural)*

herb *l'erba aromatica*
here *qui*
high blood pressure
  la pressione arteriosa elevata
high chair *il seggiolone*
high-speed train *il treno*
  ad alta velocità
hiking *l'escursionismo (m)*
hill *la collina*
him *lui: gli*
hip *l'anca (f)*
hire (verb) *noleggiare*
hockey *l'hockey (m)*
hold (verb) *tenere*
holdall *la sacca da viaggio*
holiday *la vacanza*
hood *il cappuccio*
horn *il clacson*
horse *il cavallo*
horse riding
  andare a cavallo
hospital *l'ospedale (m)*
host *il padrone di casa*
hot *caldo/a*
hot (spicy) *piccante*
hot chocolate
  la cioccolata calda
hot drinks
  le bevande calde
hotel *l'albergo (m)*
hour *l'ora (f)*
house *la casa*
hovercraft *l'hovercraft*
how *come?*
how many? *quanti/e?*
how much? *quanto/a?*
humid *umido/a*
hundred *cento*
hurricane *l'uragano (m)*
hurry (verb) *affrettarsi*
husband *il marito*
hydrant *l'idrante (m)*
hydrofoil *l'aliscafo (m)*

I

I (1st person) *io*
ice *il ghiaccio*
ice-skating
  il pattinaggio su ghiaccio
icy *ghiacciato/a*
ID *la carta d'identità*
ill *malato/a*
illness *la malattia*
immigration
  l'immigrazione (f)
in *in*
inbox *la posta in arrivo*
inch *il pollice*
infection *l'infezione (f)*
inhaler *l'inalatore (m)*
injection *l'iniezione (f)*
injure (verb) *ferirsi*
injury *la ferita*
insect repellent *il repellente*
  per gli insetti
inside *all'interno*
instructions *le istruzioni*
insurance *l'assicurazione (f)*
insurance company *l'agenzia*
  assicurativa (f)
insurance policy *la polizza*
  assicurativa
intensive care unit *il reparto*
  di terapia intensiva
interest (verb) *interessare*
interesting *interessante*
internet *l'Internet (m)*
internet café *l'internet cafè*
interpreter *l'interprete (m/f)*
into *dentro*
inventory
  l'inventario (m)
iPod *l'iPod (m)*
iron *il ferro da stiro*
ironing board
  l'asse a stiro (f)
island *l'isola (f)*

it *esso/a; lo/la; gli/le*
Italian *italiano/a*
Italy *l'Italia (f)*

J

jacket *la giacca*
jam *la marmellata*
January *gennaio*
jar *il barattolo*
jaw *la mascella*
jazz club *il jazz club*
jeans *i jeans*
jellyfish *la medusa*
jet ski *la moto d'acqua*
jet skiing *l'acquascooter*
jeweller *il gioielliere*
jewellery *la gioielleria*
jogging *il footing*
jug *la brocca*
juice *il succo*
July *luglio*
jumper *il maglione*
June *giugno*

K

kayak *il kayak*
keep straight
    andare dritto
ketchup *il ketchup*
kettle *il bollitore*
key *la chiave*
keyboard *la tastiera*
kilo *il chilo*
kilogram
    il chilogrammo
kilometre
    il chilometro
kitchen *la cucina*
knee *il ginocchio*
knife *il coltello*
knock down (verb) *colpire*
know (a fact) *sapere*
know (people) *conoscere*

L

labels *le etichette*
lake *il lago*
lamb *l'agnello (m)*
laptop *il computer portatile*
large *grande*
last *ultimo/a*
last week *la settimana scorsa*
late *tardi; in ritardo*
laugh (verb) *ridere*
launderette *la lavanderia*
lawyer *l'avvocato (m)*
leak *la perdita*
learn (verb) *imparare*
leave (verb) *lasciare; partire*
left *sinistra*
left luggage *il deposito bagagli*
leg *la gamba*
leisure *il tempo libero*
leisure activities *le
    attività del tempo libero*
lemon *il limone*
lemon grass *la citronella*
lemonade *la limonata*
length *la lunghezza*
lens *la lente*
less *meno*
letterbox *la cassetta per le lettere*
lettuce *la lattuga*
library *la biblioteca*
lid *il coperchio*
life jacket *il giubbotto di
    salvataggio*
lifebuoy *il salvagente*
lifeguard *il bagnino*
lift *l'ascensore (m)*
lift pass *il pass per lo ski-lift*
light *leggero/a*
light (noun) *la luce*
light (verb) *accendere*
light bulb *la lampadina*
lighter *l'accendino (m)*
lighthouse *il faro*

lights switch
  l'interruttore per le luci
like (verb) *piacere*
lime *il tiglio*
line *la linea*
liquid *liquido*
list *la lista*
listen (verb) *ascoltare*
litre *il litro*
little *poco; piccolo*
living room *il salotto*
load (verb) *caricare*
loan *il prestito*
local *locale*
lock *il lucchetto*
lockers *gli armadietti*
lock (verb) *chiudere a chiave*
log on (verb) *connettersi*
log out (verb) *disconnettersi*
long *lungo*
look (verb) *guardare*
lose (verb) *perdere*
lost property *l'ufficio
  oggetti smarriti (m)*
love *a zero*
love (verb) *amare*
low *basso/a*
luggage *il bagaglio*
luggage rack *il portabagagli*
lunch *il pranzo*
lunch menu *il menù del pranzo*

M

magazine *la rivista*
main course *il piatto principale*
make (verb) *fare*
make-up *il trucco*
mallet *il maglio*
man *l'uomo (m)*
manager *il capo*
mango *il mango*
manicure *la manicure*
manual *il manuale*

manuscript *il manoscritto*
many *molti/e*
map *la mappa; la cartina*
March *marzo*
marina *il porticciolo*
market *il mercato*
marmalade *la marmellata
  di agrumi*
married *sposato/a*
mascara *il mascara*
massage *il massaggio*
match (light) *il fiammifero*
match (sport) *la partita*
matt *opaco/a*
mattress *il materasso*
May *maggio*
maybe *forse*
mayonnaise *la maionese*
measure *la misura*
meat *la carne*
meatballs *le polpette*
mechanic *il meccanico*
medicine *la medicina*
medium *mezzo*
memory card *la scheda
  di memoria*
memory stick *la chiavetta USB*
mend (verb) *riparare*
menu *il menù*
message *il messaggio*
messages *i messaggi*
metal *il metallo*
metre *il metro*
microwave *il forno a microonde*
midday *mezzogiorno*
middle *mezzo*
midnight *mezzanotte*
migraine *l'emicrania (f)*
mile *il miglio*
milk *il latte*
mineral water *l'acqua
  minerale (f)*
mini bar *il mini bar*

mint *la menta*
minute *il minuto*
mirror *lo specchio*
mistake *l'errore (m)*
misty *nebbioso/a*
mixed *misto/a*
mixing bowl *l'insalatiera (f)*
mobile phone *il cellulare*
mole (medical) *il neo*
Monday *lunedì*
money *il denaro; i soldi*
monkey *la scimmia*
month *il mese*
monument *il monumento*
mooring *l'ormeggio (m)*
more *più*
morning *il mattino*
mosquito *la zanzara*
mosquito net *la zanzariera*
mother *la madre*
motorbike *la motocicletta*
motorway *l'autostrada (f)*
mountain *la montagna*
mountain bike
    la mountain bike
mouse *il topo*
mouse (computer) *il mouse*
mouth *la bocca*
mouthwash *il collutorio*
move *la mossa*
mozzarella *la mozzarella*
much *molto*
muffin *il muffin*
mug *la tazza*
muscles *i muscoli*
museum *il museo*
mushroom *il fungo*
music *la musica*
musician *il musicista*
mustard *la senape*
must (verb) *dovere*
my *mio/mia/mie/miei*
myself *mi; me stesso/a*

N

nail *l'unghia (f)*
nail clippers *i tagliaunghie*
nail scissors *le forbicine*
    per le unghie
name *il nome*
napkin *il tovagliolo*
nappy *il pannolino*
narrow *stretto*
national park *il parco nazionale*
natural *naturale*
nausea *la nausea*
navigate (verb) *navigare*
neck *il collo*
necklace *la collana*
need (verb) *aver bisogno*
nervous *nervoso/a*
net *la rete*
network *la rete*
never *mai*
new *nuovo/a*
news *il telegiornale*
newsagent *l'edicola (f)*
newspaper *il giornale*
next *prossimo/a*
next to *vicino a*
next week *la settimana prossima*
nice *bello/a; piacevole*
night *la notte*
nightclub *la discoteca*
nine *nove*
no *no*
no entry *ingresso vietato*
noisy *rumoroso/a*
normal *normale*
north *il nord*
nose *il naso*
nosebleed *il sangue dal naso*
not *non*
note *la nota*
notebook *il blocco*
notice board *il tabellone*
November *novembre*

now *adesso*
number *il numero*
number plate *il numero di targa*
nurse *l'infermiere (m)*
nursery slopes *le discese per i principianti*
nuts *le noccioline*

O

oar *il timone*
oats *l'avena (f)*
occupations *i mestieri*
occupied *occupato*
ocean *l'oceano (m)*
October *ottobre*
octopus *la piovra; il polpo*
of *di*
off *spento/a*
office *l'ufficio (m)*
often *spesso*
oil *l'olio (m)*
ointment *la pomata*
OK *d'accordo*
old *vecchio*
olive oil *l'olio d'oliva (m)*
olives *le olive*
omelette *la frittata*
on *su*
one *uno/a*
onion *la cipolla*
on (light) *acceso/a*
online *online*
only *solamente*
onto *sopra*
open *aperto/a*
open (verb) *aprire*
opening hours *l'orario di apertura (m)*
opening times *l'orario di apertura (m)*
opera *l'opera (f)*
opera house *il teatro dell'opera*

operation *l'intervento chirurgico (m)*
opposite *davanti; di fronte*
or *o*
orange (colour) *arancione*
orange juice *il succo d'arancia*
order *l'ordine (m)*
order (verb) *ordinare*
other *altro/a*
our *nostro/nostri/nostra/nostre*
outside *fuori*
oven *il forno*
oven gloves *i guanti da forno*
over *su; sopra*
overdraft *lo scoperto*
overhead locker *il compartimento portabagagli*
overnight *tutta la notte*
overtake (verb) *sorpassare*
owe (verb) *essere in debito*

P

pack (verb) *fare le valigie*
pack of cards *il mazzo di carte*
packet *il pacchetto*
pads *le ginocchiere*
pain *il dolore*
painkiller *l'antidolorifico (m)*
painting *il dipinto*
pair *la coppia*
pan *il piatto*
pan fried *fritto in padella*
pancakes *le crêpes*
paper *la carta*
papers (ID) *i documenti*
parcel *il pacco*
parents *i genitori*
park *il parco*
park (verb) *parcheggiare*
parking *il parcheggio*
parking meter *il parchimetro*
parmesan *il parmigiano*
parsley *il prezzemolo*

partner *il compagno/la compagna*
pass *il passaggio*
passenger *la passeggera*
passport *il passaporto*
passport control
  il controllo passaporti
pasta *la pasta*
pastry *le paste*
path *il viottolo*
patient *la paziente*
pause *la pausa*
pavement *il marciapiede*
pay (verb) *pagare*
pay in (verb) *effettuare un deposito*
payment *il pagamento*
payphone *il telefono pubblico*
peanut *l'arachide (f)*
peanut butter *il burro di arachidi*
pear *la pera*
pedestrian crossing
  l'attraversamento pedonale (m)
pedicure *la pedicure*
peel (verb) *sbucciare*
peeler *lo sbucciatore*
pen *la penna*
pencil *la matita*
people *la gente; le persone*
pepper *il pepe*
perfume *il profumo*
perhaps *forse*
personal CD player *il lettore CD*
pet *l'animale domestico (m)*
petrol *il carburante*
petrol station *la stazione
  di servizio*
pharmacist *il/la farmacista*
pharmacy *la farmacia*
phone *il telefono*
phone call *la telefonata*
phone card *la carta telefonica*
photo album *l'album delle
  fotografie (m)*
photo frame *la cornice*

photograph *la fotografia*
photography *la fotografia*
pianist *il/la pianista*
picnic *il picnic*
picnic hamper *il cestino da picnic*
pie *il pasticcio*
piece *il pezzo*
pilates *pilates*
pill *la compressa*
pillow *il cuscino*
pilot *il/la pilota*
PIN *il PIN*
pink *rosa*
pint *la pinta*
pitch *il campo di cricket*
pitch a tent (verb)
  piantare una tenda
pizza *la pizza*
place *il luogo*
plane *la pialla*
planet *il pianeta*
plants *le piante*
plaster *il cerotto*
plate *il piatto*
platform *il binario*
play *l'opera teatrale (f)*
play (games) (verb) *giocare*
playground *l'area giochi (f)*
please *per favore*
plug *la spina*
plum *la prugna*
plumber *l'idraulico (m)*
pocket *la tasca*
point *il punto*
poles (ski) *le racchette da sci*
police *la polizia*
police car *la volante*
police station *il commissariato*
policeman *il poliziotto*
policewoman *la poliziotta*
policy *la polizza*
pool *la piscina*
pork *il maiale*

porridge *la pappa d'avena*
porter *il facchino*
portion *la porzione*
possible *possibile*
post *la posta*
postage *l'affrancatura (f)*
postbox *la cassetta delle lettere*
postcard *la cartolina*
postman *il postino*
post office *l'ufficio postale (m)*
post (verb) *spedire la posta*
potato *la patata*
poultry *il pollame*
pound *la libbra*
pour (verb) *versare*
powder *la polvere*
power *l'elettricità (f)*
power cut *l'interruzione di corrente (f)*
prefer (verb) *preferire*
pregnancy test *il test di gravidanza*
pregnant *incinta*
prescription *la ricetta medica*
present *il regalo*
press *la stampa*
price *il prezzo*
price list *il listino*
print *la fotografia (sviluppata)*
print (photo) *la stampa*
print (verb) *stampare*
programme *il programma*
proud *fiero/a*
prove (verb) *lievitare*
province *la provincia*
public holiday *il giorno festivo*
pump (bicycle) *la pompa*
puncture *la gomma a terra*
purple *viola*
purse *il portamonete*
push *spingere*
put (verb) *mettere*
pyjamas *il pigiama*

Q, R

quarter *il quarto*
quick *rapido/a; veloce*
quite *abbastanza*
rabbit *il coniglio*
race *la gara*
racecourse *l'ippodromo (m)*
rack *la rastrelliera*
radiator *il radiatore*
radio *la radio*
rail *la rotaia*
railway *la ferrovia*
rainforest *la foresta pluviale*
raining *piovendo*
rape *la violenza carnale*
rarely *raramente*
rash *l'eruzione (f)*
raspberry *il lampone*
rat *il ratto*
raw *crudo/a*
razor *il rasoio*
read (verb) *leggere*
ready *pronto/a*
really *veramente*
receipt *la ricevuta*
receive (verb) *ricevere*
reception *la ricezione*
receptionist *l'addetto/a alla ricezione (m/f)*
reclaim tag *la ricevuta dei bagagli*
recommend (verb) *consigliare*
record *il primato*
record shop *il negozio di dischi*
recycling bin *il contenitore di riciclaggio*
red *rosso/a*
reduction *la riduzione*
refrigerator *il frigorifero*
region *la regione*
relatives *i parenti*
release (verb) *rilasciare*
remote control *il telecomando*
rent (verb) *affittare; noleggiare*

repair (verb) *riparare*
report (verb) *denunciare*
research *la ricerca*
reservation *la prenotazione*
reserve (verb) *prenotare; riservare*
rest *la pausa*
restaurant *il ristorante*
restaurant car
   la carrozza ristorante
resuscitation *la rianimazione*
retired *in pensione*
return *il ritorno*
return ticket *il biglietto di
   andata e ritorno*
reverse charge call *la chiamata
   a carico del destinatario*
reverse (verb) *fare marcia indietro*
rewind *il riavvolgimento*
rib *la costola*
rice *il riso*
rides *le giostre*
right (direction) *destra*
ring *l'anello (m)*
rinse (verb) *sciacquare*
ripe *maturo/a*
river *il fiume*
road *la strada*
roads *le strade*
road signs *segnali stradali (m pl)*
roadworks *i lavori stradali*
roast *l'arrosto (m)*
rob (verb) *derubare*
robbery *il furto*
robe *la toga*
rock climbing *l'alpinismo
   in parete (m)*
rocks *le rocce*
roll (film) *il rullino*
romance *il film d'amore*
roof *il tetto*
roofrack *il bagagliaio*
room *la stanza; la camera*
room key *la chiave della camera*

root *la radice*
rope *la corda*
rough *il rough*
round *rotondo/a*
roundabout *la rotatoria*
router *router (f)*
row *la fila*
rowing machine *il vogatore*
rubbish bin *la pattumiera*
ruby *il rubino*
rug *il tappeto*
run *il giro*
rush *il giunco*

S

sad *triste*
safari park *il parco safari*
safe *sicuro/a*
sailing *la vela*
sailing boat *la barca a vela*
salad *l'insalata (f)*
salami *il salame*
sales assistant *il commesso*
salmon *il salmone*
saloon car *la berlina*
salt *il sale*
salted *salato/a*
same *stesso/a*
sand *la sabbia*
sandals *i sandali*
sandwich *il tramezzino*
sanitary towel *l'assorbente (m)*
satellite navigation
   la navigazione via satellite
satellite TV *la TV satellitare*
satnav *il navigatore satellitare*
Saturday *sabato*
sauce *la salsa*
saucepan *la pentola*
saucer *il piattino*
sauna *la sauna*
sausage *il wurstel*
sauté (verb) *rosolare*

ave (verb) *parare*

avings account *il conto di risparmio*

avoury *salato/a*

ay (verb) *dire*

cales *la bilancia*

can *l'ecografia (f)*

cared *spaventato/a*

carf *la sciarpa*

chool *la scuola*

cissors *le forbici*

coop *la pallina*

core *lo spartito*

cuba diving *il nuoto subacqueo*

ea *il mare*

eafood *i frutti di mare*

earch (verb) *cercare*

eason *la stagione*

easons *le stagioni*

eat *il posto; la sedia*

econd *secondo/a*

econd floor *il secondo piano*

ecurity *la sicurezza*

eedless *senza semi*

eeds *i semi*

ee (verb) *vedere*

ell (verb) *vendere*

ell-by date *la data di scadenza*

end (verb) *inviare; mandare; spedire*

end off *l'espulsione (f)*

enior citizen *anziano/a*

ensitive *sensibile*

entence *la sentenza*

eparately *separatamente*

eptember *settembre*

erious *grave; serio/a*

erve *il servizio*

erve (verb) *servire*

ervices *i servizi*

et *la scenografia*

even *sette*

ew (verb) *cucire*

shampoo *lo shampoo*

shark *lo squalo*

sharp *il diesis*

shaving foam *la schiuma da barba*

she *ella; lei*

sheet *il lenzuolo*

shelf *lo scaffale*

shelves *la mensola*

shirt *la camicia*

shock *lo shock*

shoe *la scarpa*

shoes *le scarpe*

shoe shop *il negozio di calzature*

shop *il negozio*

shop assistant *la commessa*

shopping *fare la spesa*

shopping mall *il centro commerciale*

short *corto/a*

shorts *i calzoncini*

shoulder *la spalla*

shout (verb) *gridare*

shower *la doccia*

shower gel *il docciaschiuma*

shy *timida*

sick *malato/a*

side *il lato*

side effect *l'effetto indesiderato (m)*

side order *il contorno*

side plate *il piattino*

sightseeing *il giro turistico*

sign *l'insegna (f)*

signal *il segnale*

signature *la firma*

signpost *il cartello*

silk *la seta*

silver *l'argento (m)*

singer *cantante (m/f)*

single bed *il letto singolo*

single room *la camera singola*

single ticket *il biglietto di sola andata*

sink *il lavandino*
siren *la sirena*
sister *la sorella*
six *sei*
size *la taglia*
skate *il pattino*
sketch *lo schizzo*
ski *lo sci*
ski boots *gli scarponi da sci*
ski slope *la pista da sci*
skiing *lo sci*
skin *la pelle*
skirt *la gonna*
skis *gli sci*
sleeping *dormire*
sleeping bag *il sacco a pelo*
sleeping pill *il sonnifero*
slice *la fetta*
slide *lo scivolo*
slip *la sottoveste*
slippers *le pantofole*
slip road *la rampa di accesso*
sliproad *la bretella*
slope *la pendenza*
slow *lento/a*
slow down *rallentare*
small *piccolo/a*
smartphone *lo smartphone*
smash *la schiacciata*
smile *il sorriso*
smoke *il fumo*
smoke (verb) *fumare*
smoke alarm *il rivelatore di fumo*
smoking area *area fumatori*
snack *lo spuntino*
snack bar *il dolciume*
snake *il serpente*
sneeze *lo starnuto*
sneeze (verb) *starnutire*
snore (verb) *russare*
snorkel *il boccaglio*
snow *la neve*
snow (verb) *nevicare*

snowboard *lo snowboard*
snowboarding *lo snowboard*
so *così*
soak (verb) *mettere a bagno*
soap *il sapone*
soccer *il calcio*
socks *i calzini*
soda water *la soda*
sofa *il divano*
sofa bed *il divano letto*
soft *morbido/a*
soft drinks *le bibite*
soft toy *il peluche*
soil *il terreno*
some *alcuni/e*
somebody *qualcuno/a*
something *qualcosa*
sometimes *qualche volta*
son *il figlio*
song *la canzone*
soon *presto*
sorbet *il sorbetto*
sore *infiammato/a*
sorry *scusi*
soup *la minestra*
sour *agro/a*
south *il sud*
souvenir *il souvenir*
souvenirs *i ricordi*
spare tyre *la ruota di scorta*
spatula *la spatola*
speak (verb) *parlare*
speaker *l'oratore/ l'oratrice*
speciality *la specialità*
specials *le specialità*
speed limit *il limite di velocità*
speedometer *il tachimetro*
spices *le spezie*
spider *il ragno*
spinach *gli spinaci*
spine *la spina dorsale*
splint *la stecca*
splinter *la scheggia*

poke *il raggio*	strap *la spallina*
ponge *la spugna*	strawberry *la fragola*
poon *il cucchiaio*	street *la strada; la via*
port *lo sport*	street map *la strada; la mappa*
ports *gli articoli sportivi*	street sign *il segnale stradale*
ports centre *il centro sportivo*	stress *lo stress*
prain *la distorsione*	string *la corda*
pray *lo spray*	strong *forte*
pring *la primavera*	student
quare *il quadrato*	*lo studente/ la studentessa*
quare (in town) *la piazza*	student card *la carta studenti*
quash (game) *lo squash*	study *lo studio*
taff *il personale*	suburb *la periferia*
tage *il palcoscenico*	suit *il completo*
taircase *la scala*	suitcase *la valigia*
tairs *le scale*	summer *l'estate (f)*
talls *la platea*	sun *il sole*
tamp *il francobollo*	sun lounger *il lettino sdraio*
tand *il sostegno*	sunbathe (verb) *prendere il sole*
tart (verb) *cominciare*	sunbed *il lettino solare*
tarter *l'antipasto*	sunblock *la crema schermo totale*
tatement *la dichiarazione*	sunburn *la bruciatura*
tation *la stazione*	Sunday *domenica*
tatue *la statua*	sunflower oil *l'olio di*
tay *il soggiorno*	*semi di girasole*
teak *la bistecca*	sunglasses *gli occhiali da sole*
teamed *al vapore*	sunhat *il cappello da sole*
tep machine *la step machine*	sunny *assolato/a*
tew *il minestrone*	sunrise *il sorgere del sole*
tick *la mazza*	sunscreen *il filtro solare*
ting *il pungiglione*	sunset *il tramonto*
tir-fry *la frittura*	sunshine *la luce del sole*
tir (verb) *rimestare*	suntan lotion *la lozione solare*
tolen *rubato/a*	supermarket *il supermercato*
tomach *lo stomaco*	support *il supporto*
tomach ache *il mal di stomaco*	suppositories *le supposte*
tone *la pietra preziosa*	surf *la cresta dell'onda*
top *lo stop*	surf (verb) *fare surf*
top (bus) *la fermata*	surfboard *la tavola da surf*
topcock *il rubinetto di arresto*	surgeon *il/la chirurgo*
top (verb) *fermare*	surgery *l'ambulatorio (m)*
tormy *tempestoso/a*	surprised *sorpreso/a*
traight *dritto*	sweatshirt *la felpa*

sweep (verb) *spazzare*
sweet *dolce*
sweet potato *la patata dolce*
sweets *le caramelle*
swim (verb) *nuotare*
swimming *il nuoto*
swimming pool *la piscina*
swimsuit *il costume*
swing *l'altalena (f)*
switch *l'interruttore (m)*

T

table *il tavolo*
tablet *la compressa*
tailor *il sarto/la sarta*
take (verb) *prendere*
takeaway *da portar via*
take off (verb) *decollare*
tall *alto/a*
tampon *il tampone*
tan *l'abbronzatura (f)*
tank *il serbatoio*
tap *il rubinetto*
tap water *l'acqua dal rubinetto (f)*
tax *l'imposta (f)*
taxi *il taxi*
taxi driver *il/la tassista*
taxi rank *il posteggio dei taxi*
tea *il tè*
teabag *la bustina di tè*
team *la squadra*
teapot *la teiera*
teaspoon *il cucchiaino*
teeth *i denti*
telephone *il telefono*
telephone (verb) *telefonare*
telephone box *la cabina del telefono*
television (set) *il televisore*
tell (verb) *dire*
temperature *la temperatura*
ten *dieci*
tennis *il tennis*

tennis ball *la palla da tennis*
tennis court *il campo da tennis*
tennis racquet *la racchetta da tennis*
tent *la tenda*
tent peg *il picchetto*
terminal *il terminal*
test *l'analisi (f)*
text (SMS) *il messaggio (SMS)*
than *di*
thank you *grazie*
that *quello/a*
the *il/lo/la/i/gli/le*
theatre *il teatro*
their *loro*
then *poi; allora*
there *là*
there is/are *c'è/ci sono*
thermometer *il termometro*
thermostat *termostato (m)*
thick *spesso/a*
thief *ladro (m)*
thin *sottile*
think (verb) *pensare*
thirty *trenta*
this *questo/a*
thousand *mille*
three *tre*
throat *la gola*
throat lozenge *la pasticca per la gola*
through *attraverso*
throw *la proiezione*
thumb *il pollice*
Thursday *giovedì*
ticket *il biglietto*
ticket barrier *la barriera*
ticket inspector *il controllore*
ticket office *la biglietteria*
tie *la cravatta*
tight *stretto/a*
tights *il collant*
tile *la pedina*

till *la cassa*
time *il tempo*
timetable *l'orario (m)*
tip *la punta*
tissue *il fazzolettino*
toast *il pane tostato*
toaster *il tostapane*
tobacco *il tabacco*
tobacconist *il tabaccaio (m)*
today *oggi*
toe *il dito del piede*
toilet *il bagno*
toiletries *gli articoli da toeletta*
toilet roll *la carta igienica*
toll *il pedaggio*
tomato *il pomodoro*
tomato sauce *il ketchup*
tomorrow *domani*
tongue *la lingua*
tonight *stasera*
too (excessively) *troppo/a*
tooth *il dente*
toothache *il mal di denti*
toothbrush *lo spazzolino da denti*
toothpaste *il dentifricio*
torch *la torcia*
tour *il giro*
tour bus *il pullman turistico*
tour guide *la guida turistica*
tourist *il/la turista (m/f)*
tourist attraction *il luogo d'interesse turistico*
tourist information *l'ufficio informazioni turistiche (m)*
tourist information office *l'ufficio del turismo (m)*
towards *verso*
towel *l'asciugamano (m)*
towels *gli asciugamani*
town *la città*
town centre *il centro della città*
town hall *il municipio*
tow (verb) *rimorchiare*

toy *il giocattolo*
track *il binario*
traffic *il traffico*
traffic jam *l'ingorgo*
traffic lights *il semaforo*
train *il treno*
trainers *le scarpe da ginnastica*
train station *la stazione ferroviaria*
tram *il tram*
transport *i trasporti*
trash *il cestino*
travel agent *l'agente di viaggio (m)*
traveller's cheque *il travellers cheque*
travel-sickness pills *le pasticche antinausea*
tray *il vassoio*
tree *l'albero (m)*
trekking *l'escursione a cavallo (f)*
trip *la gita*
tripod *il treppiede*
trolley *il carrello*
trousers *i pantaloni*
trout *la trota*
try *la meta*
try (verb) *provare*
t-shirt *la t-shirt*
tub *la vaschetta*
tube *il tubetto*
Tuesday *martedì*
tumble dryer *l'asciuga-biancheria (f)*
tuna *il tonno*
turn off (verb) *spegnere*
turn (verb) *girare; voltare*
tweezers *la pinzetta*
twenty *venti*
twin bedded room *la camera a due letti*

twin room
 la camera a due letti
two *due*
tyre *il pneumatico*
tyre pressure
 la pressione degli pneumatici

U

ugly *brutto/a*
umbrella *l'ombrello (m)*
uncle *lo zio*
under *sotto*
underground map
 la mappa della metropolitana
underground railway
 la metropolitana
underground train
 la metropolitana
underpass *il sottopassaggio*
understand (verb)
 capire; comprendere
underwear *la biancheria intima*
uniform *l'uniforme (f)*
United States *gli Stati Uniti*
university *l'università (f)*
unleaded *senza piombo*
until *fino a*
up *su*
upset *adirato/a*
urgent *urgente*
us *noi*
useful *utile*
use (verb) *usare*
usual *solito/a*
usually *generalmente*

V

vacancy (room) *la stanza libera*
vacuum flask *il thermos*
validate (verb) *vidimare*
valuables *gli oggetti di valore*
vegetables *la verdura*
vegetarian *vegetariano/a*

veggie burger *l'hamburger
 vegetariano (m)*
venetian blind
 la tenda veneziana
very *molto*
vest *la canottiera*
vet *il veterinario/la veterinaria*
video game *il videogioco*
view *la vista*
village *il villaggio*
vinegar *l'aceto (m)*
vineyard *il vigneto*
virus *il virus*
visa *il visto*
vision *la vista*
visiting hours
 l'orario delle visite (m)
visitor *il visitatore*
vitamins *le vitamine*
voice message
 il messaggio vocale
volume *il volume*
vomit (verb) *vomitare*

W

wait (verb) *aspettare*
waiter *il cameriere*
waiting room *la sala d'attesa*
waitress *la cameriera*
wake up (verb) *svegliarsi*
wake-up call *la sveglia telefonica*
walk *la passeggiata*
walking boots *gli scarponi*
wall *il muro*
wallet *il portafoglio*
want (verb) *volere*
ward *la corsia*
wardrobe *l'armadio*
warm *caldo/a*
washing machine *la lavatrice*
wash (verb) *lavare*
wasp *la vespa*
watch *l'orologio da polso*

watch (verb) *guardare*

water *l'acqua (f)*

water bottle *la borraccia*

waterfall *la cascata*

watermelon *l'anguria*

waterproofs
gli indumenti impermeabili

water-skiing *lo sci d'acqua*

watersports *gli sport acquatici*

wave *l'onda (f)*

wax *la depilazione*

we *noi*

weak *debole*

weather *il tempo*

website *il sito web*

wedding *il matrimonio*

Wednesday *mercoledì*

week *la settimana*

weekend *il fine settimana*

weigh (verb) *pesare*

weight *il peso*

welcome *benvenuto/a*

well *bene*

wellington boots *le galosce*

west *l'ovest (m)*

wet *bagnato/a*

wet wipe
la salviettina umidificata

wetsuit *la tuta subacquea*

whale *la balena*

what? *cosa?*

wheat *il grano*

wheel *la ruota*

wheelchair *la sedia a rotelle*

wheelchair access *l'accesso per i
disabili (m)*

wheelchair ramp
la rampa per i disabili

when? *quando?*

where? *dove?*

which? *quale?*

whisk *la frusta (f)*

whisky *il whisky*

white *bianco/a*

who? *chi?*

whole *intero*

why? *perché?*

wide *largo/a*

widescreen TV *il televisore
a schermo panoramico*

width *la larghezza*

Wi-Fi *Wifi*

wife *la moglie*

win (verb) *vincere*

wind *il vento*

window *la finestra*

window seat *il posto
vicino al finestrino*

windscreen *la parabrezza*

windscreen wiper
il tergicristallo

windsurfer *il/la surfista (m/f)*

windy *ventoso/a*

wine *il vino*

wine glass *il calice da vino*

wine list *la lista dei vini*

winter *l'inverno (m)*

winter sports *gli sport invernali*

wipe (verb) *pulire*

wiper blades *le spazzole del
tergicristallo*

with *con*

withdraw (money) (verb)
prelevare

withdrawal *il prelievo*

without *senza*

witness *il/la testimone (m/f)*

woman *la donna*

wood *il bosco*

wool *la lana*

work *il lavoro*

work (machine) *funzionare*

work (verb) *lavorare*

worried *preoccupato/a*

worse *peggiore*

wrap (a gift) *incartare*

wrapping paper
  la carta da regalo
wrist *il polso*
wrist watch *l'orologio da polso*
write (verb) *scrivere*
wrong *sbagliato/a*

X, Y, Z

X-ray *la radiografia*
yacht *lo yacht*
year *l'anno (m)*

yellow *giallo/a*
yes *sì*
yesterday *ieri*
yoga *lo yoga*
yoghurt *lo yogurt*
you *Lei; tu (singular); voi (plural)*
young *giovane*
zero *zero*
zip *la chiusura lampo*
zone *la zona*
zoo *lo zoo*

The gender of Italian nouns is shown by the abbreviations (m) for masculine and (f) for feminine. Plural nouns are followed by the abbreviations (m pl) or (f pl). Adjectives vary according to the gender and number of the word they describe. Here the masculine singular form (usually "o") is shown, followed by the alternative feminine ending (usually "a").

A

a *at*

abbastanza *quite*

abbigliamento (m) *clothing*

abbronzatura (f) *tan*

abiti (m pl) *clothes*

abito (m) *dress*

abito da sera (m)
evening dress

accamparsi *to camp*

accappatoio (m)
bath robe

accendere *to light*

accendino (m) *lighter*

acceso *on (light)*

accesso per i disabili (m)
wheelchair access

aceto (m) *vinegar*

acqua (f) *water*

acqua dal rubinetto (f)
tap water

acqua in bottiglia (f)
bottled water

acqua minerale (m)
mineral water

acquascooter (m)
jet skiing

adattatore (m) *adapter*

addebitare *to charge*

addebito diretto (m)
direct debit

addetta alla ricezione (f)
receptionist

adesso *now*

a destra (f) *right*

adirato *upset*

adulto (m) *adult*

aerobica (f) *aerobics*

aeroplano (m) *aeroplane*

aeroporto (m) *airport*

affittare *to rent*

affrancatura (f) *postage*

affrettarsi *to hurry*

agenda (f) *diary*

agente di viaggio (m)
travel agent

agenzia assicurativa (f)
insurance company

agenzia immobiliare (f)
estate agent's

aglio (m) *garlic*

agnello (m) *lamb*

agosto *August*

agricoltore (m) *farmer*

agro *sour*

agrumi (m pl) *citrus fruit*

airbag (m) *airbag*

aiutare *to help*

aiuto (m) *help*

albergo (m) *hotel*

albero (m) *tree*

albicocca (f) *apricot*

album delle fotografie (m)
photo album

alcuni/e *some*
aliscafo (m) *hydrofoil*
allarme antincendio (m)
   fire alarm
allegato (m) *attachment*
allergia (f) *allergy*
allergico/a *allergic*
all'interno *inside*
alloggio (m) *accommodation*
allora *then*
alpinismo in parete (m)
   rock climbing
altalena (f) *swing*
altezza (f) *height*
alto *tall*
altro/a *other;*
   un altro/un'altra *another*
al vapore *steamed*
amaro *bitter*
ambasciata (f) *embassy*
ambulanza (f) *ambulance*
ambulatorio (m)
   doctor's surgery
amico/a (m/f) *friend*
analisi (f) *test*
analisi del sangue (f pl)
   blood test
anatra (f) *duck*
anche *too (also)*
ancora *again*
andare *to go*
andare a cavallo *horse riding*
andare dritto *to go straight*
andare in bici *to cycle*
andare in discoteca
   to go clubbing
anello (m) *ring*
anguria (f) *watermelon*
animale domestico (m) *pet*
animali (m pl) *animals*
anno (m) *year*
annoiato *bored*
antibiotici (m pl) *antibiotics*

antidolorifico (m) *painkiller*
antipasto (m) *starter*
anziano/a (m/f)
   senior citizen
ape (f) *bee*
aperto/a *open*
appartamento (m)
   apartment
appendiabiti (m)
   coat hanger
applaudire *to applaud*
applicazione (f)
   application
appuntamento (m)
   appointment
apribottiglie (m)
   bottle/can opener
aprile *April*
aprire *to open*
arachide (f) *peanut*
arancione *orange (colour)*
architetto (m) *architect*
architettura (f) *architecture*
arco (m) *arc*
arco plantare (m) *arch*
area fumatori (f)
   smoking area
area giochi (f) *playground*
argento (m) *silver*
aria condizionata (f) *air*
   conditioning
armadietti (m pl) *lockers*
armadio (m) *wardrobe*
arrabbiata *angry*
arrangiamenti (m pl)
   arrangements
arrivare *to arrive*
arrivederci *goodbye*
arrivi (m pl) *arrivals hall*
arrosto (m) *roast*
arte (f) *art*
articoli da toeletta
   (m pl) *toiletries*

articoli sportivi (m pl) *sports*
artista (m/f) *artist*
artrite (f) *arthritis*
ascensore (m) *lift*
asciuga-biancheria (f)
  tumble dryer
asciugacapelli (m)
  hairdryer
asciugamani (m pl)
  towels
asciugamano (m) *towel*
asciugamano grande (m)
  bath towel
asciugare con il fon
  to blow dry
asciutto *dry (day; clothes)*
ascoltare *to listen*
asma (f) *asthma*
a sinistra *left*
aspettare *to wait*
aspetto (m) *appearance*
asse da stiro (f)
  ironing board
assegno (m) *cheque*
assicurazione (f) *insurance*
assicurazione sanitaria (f)
  health insurance
assistente (m/f) *assistant*
assistente di volo (m/f)
  air stewardess
assolato/a *sunny*
assorbente (m)
  sanitary towel
atleta (m) *athlete*
atrio (m) *concourse*
attaccante (m) *forward*
attacco (m) *attack*
attenzione (f) *caution*
attività (f pl) *activites*
attore (m) *actor*
attorno *around*
attraversamento pedonale (m)
  pedestrian crossing

attraverso *through*
attrezzatura (f) *equipment*
attrice (f) *actress*
audio guida (f) *audio guide*
Australia (f) *Australia*
autista (m/f) *driver*
autobus (m) *bus*
autolavaggio (m)
  car wash
automatico *automatic*
automobile (f) *car*
autonoleggio (m)
  car rental
autopompa (f) *fire engine*
autostrada (f) *motorway*
autunno (m) *autumn*
avena (f) *oats*
aver bisogno *to need*
avere *to have*
avocado (m) *avocado*
avvocato (m) *lawyer*
a zero *love*

B

bacca (f) *berry*
badminton (m) *badminton*
bagaglio (m) *luggage*
bagagliaio (m) *boot*
  (car); roofrack
bagaglio a mano (m)
  hand luggage
bagaglio consentito (m)
  baggage allowance
bagel (m) *bagel*
bagnato/a *wet*
bagnino (m) *lifeguard*
bagno (m) *bath;*
  bathroom; toilet
bagnoschiuma (m)
  bubblebath
balcone (m) *balcony*
balena (f) *whale*
ballare *dancing*

balsamo (m) *conditioner*
bambini (m pl) *children*
bambino/a (m/f) *child*
bambola (f) *doll*
banana (f) *banana*
banca (f) *bank*
banco accettazione (m)
  check-in desk
bancomat (m) *ATM*
bandierina (f) *flag*
bar (m) *bar; café*
barattolo (m) *jar*
barbabietola (f) *beetroot*
barbecue (m) *barbecue*
barbiere (m) *barber*
barca (f) *boat*
barca a vela (f) *sailing boat*
barista (m) *bartender*
barriera (f) *ticket barrier*
barriera corallina (f)
  coral reef
baseball (m) *baseball*
basilico (m) *basil*
basso *low*
batteria (f) *battery*
bello/a *beautiful; nice*
bemolle (m) *flat*
benda (f) *bandage*
bene *alright; well*
benvenuto *welcome*
bere *to drink*
berlina (f) *saloon car*
bevande alcoliche (f pl)
  alcoholic drinks
bevande calde (f pl)
  hot drinks
biancheria da letto (f)
  bed linen
biancheria intima (f)
  underwear
bianco/a *white*
bibita (f) *drink (noun)*
bibite (f pl) *drinks*

biblioteca (f) *library*
bicchiere (m) *glass (drinking)*
bicicletta (f) *bicycle;*
  exercise bike
bidet (m) *bidet*
biglietteria (f) *ticket office*
biglietteria automatica (f)
  automatic ticket machine
biglietto (m) *ticket*
biglietto d'auguri (m) *card*
biglietto d'entrata (m)
  entrance ticket
biglietto di andata e ritorno (m)
  return ticket
biglietto di sola andata (m)
  single ticket
biglietto famiglia (m)
  family ticket
bikini (m) *bikini*
bilancia (f) *scales*
bimbo (m) *baby*
binario (m) *platform*
biondo *blonde*
birra (f) *beer*
biscotto (m) *biscuit*
blatta (f) *cockroach*
blocco (m) *notebook*
blu *blue*
boa (f) *buoy*
bocca (f) *mouth*
boccaglio (m) *snorkel*
bollire *to boil*
bollitore (m) *camping kettle;*
  kettle
bonifico (m) *bank transfer*
bordo; a bordo *on board*
borraccia (f) *water bottle*
borsa (f) *bag; handbag*
borsa da viaggio (f) *holdall*
borsa per fotocamera (f)
  camera bag
bosco (m) *wood*
bottiglia (f) *bottle*

bottone (m) *button*
boutique (f) *boutique*
bowling (m) *bowling*
bracciale (m) *bracelet*
braccio (m) *arm*
bretella (f) *sliproad*
brioche (f) *brioche*
britannico/a *British*
brocca (f) *jug*
broccolo (m) *broccoli*
bruciatura (f) *burn*
bruno/a *brunette*
brutto/a *ugly*
buffet (m) *buffet*
buffet della colazione (m)
  breakfast buffet
bulbo (m) *bulb*
Buon pomeriggio
  good afternoon
buonanotte *good night*
buonasera *good evening*
buongiorno *hello*
Buongiorno *good morning*
buono/a *good*
burro (m) *butter*
burro di arachidi (m)
  peanut butter
bussola (f) *compass*
busta (f) *envelope*
bustina di tè (f) *teabag*
busto (m) *bust*

C

cabina (f) *cabin*
cabina del telefono (f)
  telephone box
caffè (m) *coffee*
caffè nero (m) *black coffee*
caffettiera (f) *cafetière*
calcio (m) *football (game)*
calcio d'angolo (m) *corner*
calcolatrice (f) *calculator*
caldo/a *hot; warm*

calendario (m) *calendar*
calice da vino (m)
  wine glass
calmo/a *calm*
calzini (m pl) *socks*
calzoncini (m pl) *shorts*
cambiare *to change*
camera (f) *room*
camera a due letti (f)
  twin room
camera da letto (f)
  bedroom
camera doppia (f)
  double room
camera familiare (f)
  family room
camera singola (f)
  single room
cameriera (f) *waitress*
cameriere (m) *waiter*
camerini (m pl)
  changing rooms
camicetta (f) *blouse*
camicia (f) *shirt*
camminare *to walk*
campanello (m) *doorbell*
campeggiare *to camp*
campeggio (m) *campsite*
camper (m) *caravan*
campo (m) *field*
campo da golf (m)
  golf course
campo da tennis (m)
  tennis court
campo di cricket (m) *pitch*
Canada (m) *Canada*
canale di scolo (m) *drain*
canale (m) *channel (TV)*
cancello (m) *gate*
candeggina (f) *bleach*
cane (m) *dog*
canna da pesca (f)
  fishing rod

cannella (f) *cinnamon*

canoa (f) *canoe*

canottiera (f) *vest*

cantante (m/f) *singer*

cantiere (m) *building site*

canzone (f) *song*

capelli (m pl) *hair*

capire *to understand*

capitale (f) *capital*

capo (m) *manager*

cappello (m) *hat*

cappello da sole (m) *sunhat*

cappotto (m) *coat*

cappuccino (m) *cappuccino*

cappuccio (m) *hood*

capsula (f) *capsule*

caramelle (f pl) *sweets*

carburante (m) *petrol*

cardigan (m) *cardigan*

caricare *to load*

carne (f) *meat*

carnevale (m) *carnival*

caro/a *expensive*

carota (f) *carrot*

carrello (m) *trolley*

carrozza ristorante (f) *dining car*

carta assegni (f) *cheque card*

carta di credito (f) *credit card*

carta di debito (f) *debit card*

carta d'identità (f) *ID*

carta d'imbarco (f) *boarding pass*

carta igienica (f) *toilet roll*

carta studenti (f) *student card*

carta telefonica (f) *phone card*

carte (f pl) *cards*

cartelli stradali (m pl) *road signs*

cartello (m) *signpost*

cartina (f) *map; street map*

cartolina (f) *postcard*

cartone (m) *cardboard*

casa (f) *house*

cascata (f) *waterfall*

casco (m) *cycling helmet*

casinò (m) *casino*

cassa (f) *till*

cassa (f) *check-out (supermarket)*

casseruola (f) *casserole dish*

cassetta delle lettere (f) *postbox*

cassetta di pronto soccorso (f) *first-aid box*

cassetta per le lettere (f) *letterbox*

cassetto (m) *drawer*

cassiere/a (m/f) *cashier*

castello (m) *castle*

casual *casual*

catamarano (m) *catamaran*

cattedrale (f) *cathedral*

cattivo/a *bad*

cavalletto (m) *bike rack*

cavallo (m) *horse*

cavatappi (m) *corkscrew*

caverna (f) *cave*

caviglia (f) *ankle*

cavolfiore (m) *cauliflower*

cavo (m) *cable*

cavolo (m) *cabbage*

CD (m) *CD*

c'è *there is*

ceci (m pl) *chickpeas*

cellulare (m) *mobile phone*

cena (f) *dinner*

cento *hundred*

centro commerciale (m) *shopping mall*

centro della città (m) *town centre*
centro sportivo (m) *sports centre*
cercare *to search*
cerchio (m) *circle*
cereale (m) *cereal*
cereali da colazione (m pl) *breakfast cereals*
cerotto (m) *plaster*
certificato di nascita (m) *birth certificate*
cervello (m) *brain*
cestino (m) *trash*
cestino (m) *basket*
cestino da picnic (m) *picnic hamper*
cetriolo (m) *cucumber*
champagne (m) *champagne*
check-in (m) *check in*
chi? *who?*
chiamata a carico del destinatario (f) *reverse charge call*
chiave (f) *key*
chiave della camera (f) *room key*
chiavetta USB (f) *memory stick*
chicchi (m pl) *beans*
chiesa (f) *church*
chilogrammo (m) *kilogram*
chilo (m) *kilo*
chilometro (m) *kilometre*
chirurgo (m) *surgeon*
chiudere *to close*
chiudere a chiave *to lock*
chiuso/a *closed*
chiusura lampo (f) *zip*
chorizo (m) *chorizo*
ciao *hello*
ciascuno *each*
cibo (m) *food*
ciglio (m) *eyelash*

ciliegia (f) *cherry*
cin cin! *cheers!*
cinema (m) *cinema*
cinquanta *fifty*
cinque *five*
cintura (f) *belt*
cioccolata calda (f) *hot chocolate*
cioccolatino (m) *chocolate*
cipolla (f) *onion*
circa *about*
ci sono *there are*
citronella (f) *lemon grass*
città (f) *city; town*
clacson (m) *horn*
il/la cliente (m/f) *client*
clinica (f) *clinic*
cocktail (m) *cocktail*
cofano (m) *bonnet (car)*
coincidenza (f) *connection*
colazione (f) *breakfast*
coleottero (m) *beetle*
colino (m) *colander*
colla (f) *glue*
collana (f) *necklace*
collant (m) *tights*
collezione *collection*
collina (f) *hill*
collo (m) *neck*
collutorio (m) *mouthwash*
colori (m pl) *colours*
colpire *to knock down*
coltello (m) *knife*
come *as; how; like*
come? *how*
commessa (f) *shop assistant*
commesso (m) *sales assistant*
commissariato (m) *police station*
commissione bancaria (f) *bank charge*

il/la compagno/a (m/f)
  partner
compartimento portabagagli (m)
  overhead locker
compleanno (m) *birthday*
completo (m) *suit*
comporre *to dial*
comprare *to buy*
comprendere *to understand*
compressa (f) *pill; tablet*
computer (m) *computer*
computer portatile (m)
  laptop
con *with*
concerto (m) *concert*
condominio (m)
  apartment block
confuso/a *confused*
congelato/a *frozen*
coniglio (m) *rabbit*
connettersi *to log on*
conoscere *to know (people)*
consigliare *to recommend*
consolato (m) *consulate*
console (m) *consul*
contare *to count*
contenitore (m) *container*
contenitore di riciclaggio
  (m) *recycling bin*
contento/a *happy*
contenuto (m) *contents*
continente (m) *continent*
conto (m) *bill*
conto bancario (m)
  bank account
conto corrente (m)
  current account
conto di risparmio (m)
  savings account
contorno (m) *side order*
contraccezione (f)
  contraception
controllo (m) *checkup*

controllo passaporti (m)
  passport control
controllore (m) *ticket inspector*
coperchio (m) *lid*
coperta (f) *blanket*
copiare *to copy*
coppia (f) *pair*
corda (f) *string*
coriandolo (m) *coriander*
cornetto (m) *croissant*
cornice (f) *photo frame*
corpetto (m) *camisole*
corpo (m) *body*
corriere (m) *courier*
corsia (f) *aisle*
corsia (f) *ward*
cortile (m) *courtyard*
corto *short*
cosa? *what?*
così *so*
costa (f) *coast*
costola (f) *rib*
costoletta (f) *chop*
costruire *to build*
costume (m) *swimsuit*
cotone (m) *cotton*
crampo (m) *cramp*
cravatta (f) *tie*
crema (f) *cream*
crema per il corpo (f) *body lotion*
crema schermo totale (f) *sunblock*
crêpes (f pl) *pancakes*
cresta dell'onda (f) *surf*
crosta (f) *crust*
crudo *raw*
cruscotto (m) *dashboard*
cuccetta (f) *couchette*
cucchiaino (m) *teaspoon*
cucchiaio (m) *spoon*
cucina (f) *kitchen*
cucinare *cooking*
cucire *to sew*
cuffia (f) *cap*

cuffie (f pl) *headphones*
cugino/a (m/f) *cousin*
cuocere al forno *to bake*
cuocere alla griglia *to grill*
cuoco/a (m/f) *chef*
cuore (m) *heart*
curry (m) *curry*
cuscino (m) *pillow*
custodia (f) *case*

D

da *by; from*
da asporto *take-away*
d'accordo *OK*
danneggiato/a *damaged*
danza (f) *ballet*
dare *to give*
dare la precedenza
  to give way
data di scadenza (f)
  sell-by date
davanti *front;*
  in front of; opposite
debole *weak*
decollare *to take off (clothes)*
delfino (m) *dolphin*
delizioso/a *delicious*
denaro (m) *cash; money*
dente (m) *tooth*
denti (m pl) *teeth*
dentifricio (m) *toothpaste*
il/la dentista (m/f) *dentist*
dentro *into*
denuncia (f) *report (noun)*
denunciare *to report*
deodorante (m) *deodorant*
depilazione (f) *wax*
depositare *to deposit*
deposito (m) *deposit*
deposito bagagli (m)
  left luggage
derubare *to rob*
deserto (m) *desert*

dessert (m) *dessert*
destinazione (f) *destination*
destra: a destra *right (direction)*
detergente (m) *detergent*
detestare *to hate*
di *of; than*
diabetico/a *diabetic*
diarrea (f) *diarrhoea*
dicembre *December*
dichiarazione (f)
  statement
dieci *ten*
diesel *diesel*
diesis (m) *sharp*
dietro a *behind*
difficile *difficult*
digitare *to key*
dipartimento (m)
  department
dipinto (m) *painting*
dire *to say; to tell*
direttore della banca (m)
  bank manager
disabile (m) *disabled person*
discese per i principianti (f pl)
  nursery slopes
discipline (f pl) *events*
disco DVD (m) *DVD*
disconnettersi *to log out*
discutere *to discuss*
disegnare *to draw*
disegno (m) *drawing*
disinfettante (m) *antiseptic*
distanza (f) *distance*
distorsione (f) *sprain*
distretto (m) *district*
dito (m) *finger*
dito del piede (m) *toe*
ditta (f) *company*
divano (m) *sofa*
divano letto (m) *sofa bed*
divorziato/a *divorced*
dizionario (m) *dictionary*

doccia (f) *shower*
docciaschiuma (m)
   shower gel
documenti (m pl)
   papers (identity)
dodici *twelve*
dogana (f pl) *customs*
dolce *sweet; dessert*
dolci (m pl) *cakes*
dolcificante (m)
   artificial sweetener
dolciume (m) *snack bar*
dolore (m) *pain*
domani *tomorrow*
domenica *Sunday*
donna (f) *woman*
dopo *after*
doposole (m) *aftersun*
dormire *sleeping*
dorso del piede (m)
   bridge
dosaggio (m) *dosage*
dottore (m) *doctor*
dove? *where?*
dovere *to have to;*
   must (verb)
dritto (m) *straight*
due *two*
durante *during*
duro *hard*

E

e *and*
ecografia (f) *scan*
edicola (f) *newsagent*
effetto indesiderato (m)
   side effect
effettuare un deposito
   to pay in
egli *he*
elettricista (m) *electrician*
elettricità (f) *electricity*
ella *she*

ellittica (f) *cross trainer*
e-mail (f) *email*
ematoma (m) *bruise*
emergenza (f) *emergency*
emicrania (f) *migraine*
emigrare *to emigrate*
entrata (f) *entrance*
entusiasta *excited*
epilettico/a *epileptic*
erba aromatica (f) *herb*
errore (m) *mistake*
eruzione (f) *rash*
esaminare *to examine*
esattamente *exactly*
esatto/a *right (correct)*
escoriazione (f) *graze*
escursione a cavallo (f)
   trekking
escursionismo (m) *hiking*
esposizione (f) *exhibition*
espresso (m) *espresso*
espulsione (f) *send off*
essere *to be*
essere in debito *to owe*
esso/a *it*
est (m) *east*
estate (f) *summer*
estintore (m)
   fire extinguisher
etichette (f pl) *labels*
euro (m) *euro*
extra *extra*

F

facchino (m) *porter*
facile *easy*
famiglia (f) *family*
fard (m) *blusher*
fare *to do; to make*
fare il check-in *to check in*
fare la spesa *to go shopping*
fare le valigie *to pack*
fare marcia indietro *to reverse*

fare surf *to surf*
fari (m pl) *headlights*
farmacia (f) *pharmacy*
farmacista (m) *pharmacist*
faro (m) *lighthouse*
fasciatura (f) *dressing*
fast food (m) *fast food*
fattoria (f) *farm*
fazzolettino (m) *tissue*
febbraio *February*
febbre (f) *fever*
felice *happy*
felpa (f) *sweatshirt*
ferita (f) *injury*
fermare *to stop*
fermata dell'autobus (f)
  bus stop
ferramenta (f)
  hardware shop
ferrovia (f) *railway*
festa (f) *celebration*
feste (f pl) *festivals*
fetta (f) *slice*
fiammifero (m)
  match (light)
fibbia (f) *buckle*
fidanzata (f) *girlfriend*
fidanzato (m) *boyfriend*
fiero/a *proud*
figlia (f) *daughter*
figlio (m) *son*
fila (f) *row*
filetto (m) *fillet*
film d'amore (m) *romance*
filone (m) *baguette*
filtro solare (m)
  sunscreen
fine (f) *end*
fine settimana (m)
  weekend
finestra (f) *window*
finire *to finish*
fino a *until*

fioraio/a (m/f) *florist*
fiore (m) *club*
fiori (m pl) *flowers*
firma (f) *signature*
firmare *to sign*
fitness (m) *fitness*
fiume (m) *river*
flash (m) *flash gun*
fontana (f) *fountain*
footing (m) *jogging*
forbici (f pl) *scissors*
forbicine per le unghie (f pl)
  nail scissors
forchetta (f) *fork*
foresta (f) *forest*
foresta pluviale (f) *rainforest*
formaggio (m) *cheese*
formaggio cremoso (m)
  cream cheese
fornetto da campeggio (m)
  camping stove
forno (m) *oven*
forno a microonde (m)
  microwave
forse *perhaps*
forte *strong*
fotocamera digitale (f)
  digital camera
fotocamera (f) *camera*
fotografia (f) *photograph*
fotografia (sviluppata) (f)
  print
fotografia con il flash (f)
  flash photography
fragile *fragile*
fragola (f) *strawberry*
francobollo (m) *stamp*
fratello (m) *brother*
frattura (f) *fracture*
frecce lampeggianti (f pl)
  hazard lights
freddo/a *cold*
freno (m) *brake*

fresco/a *fresh*
friggere *to fry*
frigo portatile (m) *coolbox*
frigorifero (m) *refrigerator*
frigorifero congelatore (m)
  fridge-freezer
frittata (f) *omelette*
fritto *fried*
fritto in olio abbondante
  deep-fried
fritto in padella *pan fried*
frittura (f) *stir-fry*
fronte; di fronte a *front;*
  in front of; opposite
frullatore (m) *blender*
frusta (f) *whisk*
frutta (f) *fruit*
frutti di mare (m pl)
  seafood
fruttivendolo (m) *greengrocer*
fumare *to smoke*
fumetto (m) *comic*
fumo (m) *smoke*
fungo (m) *mushroom*
funivia (f) *cable car*
funzionare *to work (machine)*
fuori *outside*
furto (m) *robbery*

G

galleria (f) *gallery (theatre)*
galleria d'arte (f) *art gallery*
galosce (f pl)
  wellington boots
gamba (f) *leg*
gara (f) *race*
garage (m) *garage*
garanzia (f) *guarantee*
gas (m) *gas*
gastronomia (f) *delicatessen*
gatto (m) *cat*
gelato/a (m/f) *freeze*
gelo (m) *frost*

gemelli (m pl) *cufflinks*
generalmente *usually*
genitori (m pl) *parents*
gennaio *January*
gente (f) *people*
ghiacciato/a *icy*
ghiaccio (m) *ice*
già *already*
giacca (f) *jacket*
giaccone (m) *anorak*
giallo/a *yellow*
giardino (m) *garden*
gin (m) *gin*
ginocchiere (f pl) *pads*
ginocchio (m) *knee*
giocare *to play (games)*
giocattolo (m) *toy*
gioco (m) *game*
gioielleria (f) *jewellery*
gioielliere (m) *jeweller*
giornale (m) *newspaper*
giorno (m) *day*
giorno festivo (m)
  bank holiday
giostre (f pl) *rides*
giovane *young*
giovedì *Thursday*
giraffa (f) *giraffe*
giro (m) *run*
giro (m) *tour*
giro turistico (m) *sightseeing*
gita (f) *trip*
giù *down*
giubbotto di salvataggio
  (m) *life jacket*
giugno *June*
giunco (m) *rush*
giusto/a *right (correct)*
gli *the (m pl)*
gola (f) *throat*
golf (m) *golf*
gomito (m) *elbow*
gomma a terra (f) *puncture*

gomma da masticare (f)
chewing gum
gonna (f) *skirt*
gradi *degrees*
grammo (m) *gram*
Gran Bretagna (f) *Great Britain*
granchio (m) *crab*
grande *big; large*
grande magazzino (m)
department store
grandine (f) *hail*
grano (m) *wheat*
grasso (m) *fat*
gratis *free (no charge)*
grattugia (f) *grater*
grave *serious*
grazie *thank you*
grembiule (m) *apron*
gridare *to shout*
grigio *grey*
griglia (f) *grill pan*
griglia per barbecue (f)
barbecue
gruppo (m) *group*
guancia (f) *cheek*
guanti (m pl) *gloves*
guanti da forno (m pl)
oven gloves
guanto da baseball (m)
baseball mitt
guardacoste (m)
coastguard
guardare *to look;*
to watch
guasto (m) *breakdown*
guida (f) *guide; guidebook*
guida turistica (f) *tour guide*
guidare *to drive*

H, I, J, K

hamburger (m) *burger*
hamburger vegetariano (m)
veggie burger

hockey (m) *hockey*
hovercraft (m) *hovercraft*
i *the (m pl)*
ieri *yesterday*
idrante (m) *hydrant*
idraulico (m) *plumber*
il *the (m)*
imbarazzata *embarrassed*
imbarcarsi *to board*
imbarcazione da diporto
(f) *pleasure boat*
l'immigrazione (f)
immigration
imparare *to learn*
impianto di riscaldamento
(m) *heater*
impianto stereo dell' automobile
(m) *car stereo*
importo (m) *amount*
imposta (f) *tax*
imputazione (f) *charge*
in *in*
in stato interessante
pregnant
inalatore (m) *inhaler*
incartare *to gift-wrap*
incassare *to cash*
incendio (m) *fire*
incidente (m) *accident*
incidente stradale (m)
car accident
incinta *pregnant*
incisione (f) *engraving*
indicatore di livello del
carburante (m) *fuel gauge*
Indicazioni (f) *directions*
indirizzo (m) *address*
indirizzo e-mail (m)
email address
indumenti impermeabili
(m pl) *waterproofs*
infermiere/a (m/f)
nurse

infezione (f) *infection*
infiammato/a *sore*
influenza (f) *flu*
infradito (f) *flip-flop*
infreddatura (f) *chill*
inglese *English*
ingorgo (m) *traffic jam*
Ingresso vietato (m)
  no entry
iniezione (f) *injection*
inizio (m) *beginning*
inondazione (f) *flood*
insalata (f) *salad*
insalatiera (f) *mixing bowl*
insegna (f) *sign*
interessante *interesting*
interessare *to interest*
Internet (m) *internet*
Internet cafè (m) *internet café*
intero *whole*
interprete (m/f) *interpreter*
interruttore (m) *switch*
interruttore per le luci (m)
  lights switch
interruzione di corrente (f)
  power cut
intervento chirurgico (m)
  operation (medical)
inventario (m) *inventory*
inverno (m) *winter*
inviare *to send*
isola (f) *island*
iPod (m) *iPod*
ippodromo (m)
  racecourse
istruzioni (f pl)
  instructions
Italia (f) *Italy*
italiano/a *Italian*
jazz club (m) *jazz club*
jeans (m pl) *jeans*
kayak (m) *kayak*
ketchup (m) *ketchup*

L

la *the (f)*
là *over there*
ladro (m) *thief*
lago (m) *lake*
lampadina (f) *light bulb*
lampone (m) *raspberry*
lana (f) *wool*
larghezza (f) *width*
largo *wide*
lasciare *to check out
  (hotel); to leave; to vacate*
lassù *up there*
lato (m) *side*
latte (m) *milk*
latticini (m pl) *dairy*
lattuga (f) *lettuce*
lavanderia (f) *launderette*
lavandino (m) *sink*
lavare *to wash*
lavastoviglie (f)
  dishwasher
lavatrice (f) *washing machine*
lavorare *to work*
lavori stradali (m pl)
  roadworks
lavoro (m) *work;*
  per lavoro *on business*
le *the (f pl)*
leggere *to read*
leggero/a *light*
le *her (object)*
lei *she;* Lei *you*
lente (f) *lens*
lenti a contatto (f pl)
  contact lenses
lento/a *slow*
lenzuolo (m) *sheet*
lettino (m) *cot*
lettino sdraio (m)
  sun lounger
lettino solare (m) *sunbed*
letto (m) *bed*

letto matrimoniale (m) *double bed*

letto singolo (m) *single bed*

lettore CD (m) *CD player*

lettore DVD (m) *DVD player*

leva del cambio (f) *gear stick*

libbra (f) *pound*

libero/a *free (not occupied)*

libreria (f) *book shop*

libretto degli assegni (m) *chequebook*

libro (m) *book*

lievitare *to prove*

limite di velocità (m) *speed limit*

limonata (f) *lemonade*

limone (m) *lemon*

linea (f) *line*

lingua (f) *tongue*

liquido *liquid*

lista (f) *list*

lista dei vini (f) *wine list*

listino (m) *price list*

litro (m) *litre*

lo *the (m)*

locale *local*

lontano *far*

l'oratrice (f) *speaker*

loro *their; they*

lozione solare (f) *suntan lotion*

lucchetto (m) *lock*

luce (f) *light (noun)*

luce del sole (f) *sunshine*

lucido *gloss*

luglio *July*

lui *he; him*

luna park (m) *fairground*

lunedì *Monday*

lunghezza (f) *length*

lungo/a *long*

luoghi d'interesse (m pl) *attractions*

luogo (m) *place*

luogo d'interesse turistico (m) *tourist attraction*

M

macchina (f) *car; machine*

macchina del caffè (f) *coffee machine*

macelleria (f) *butcher's*

macinato (?) *ground*

madre (f) *mother*

maggio *May*

maglio (m) *mallet*

maglione (m) *jumper*

mai *never*

maiale (m) *pork*

maionese (f) *mayonnaise*

mais (m) *corn*

mal di denti (m) *toothache*

mal di stomaco *stomach ache*

mal di testa (m) *headache*

malato/a *ill*

malattia (f) *illness*

mandare *to send*

mangiare *to eat*

mangiare fuori *eating out*

mangiare sul posto *eat-in*

mango (m) *mango*

manicure (f) *manicure*

maniglia (f) *handle*

mano (f) *hand*

manoscritto (m) *manuscript*

manzo (m) *beef*

mappa (f) *map; street map*

mappa della metropolitana (f) *underground map*

marciapiede (m) *pavement*

mare (m) *sea*

marito (m) *husband*

marmellata (f) *jam*

marmellata di agrumi (f) *marmalade*

marmitta (f) *exhaust (car)*
marrone *brown*
martedì *Tuesday*
marzo *March*
mascara (m) *mascara*
mascella (f) *jaw*
massaggio (m) *massage*
materasso (m) *mattress*
matita (f) *pencil*
matita per gli occhi (f)
  eyeliner
matrimonio (m) *wedding*
mattino (m) *morning*
mattone (m) *brick*
maturo/a *ripe*
mazza (f) *golf club*
mazzetto (m) *bunch*
mazzo di carte (m)
  pack of cards
meccanico (m) *mechanic*
medicina (f) *medicine*
medicina per la tosse (f)
  cough medicine
medusa (f) *jellyfish*
mela (f) *apple*
melanzana (f) *aubergine*
meno *less*
mensola (f) *shelves*
menta (f) *mint*
mento (m) *chin*
menù (m) *menu*
menù della cena (m)
  evening menu
menù del pranzo (m)
  lunch menu
mercato (m) *market*
mercoledì *Wednesday*
merluzzo (m) *cod*
mese (m) *month*
messaggi (pl) *messages*
messaggio (m) *message*
messaggio vocale (m)
  voice message

metà *half*
meta (f) *try*
metallo (m) *metal*
metro (m) *metre*
metropolitana (f)
  underground railway
mettere *to put*
mezzanotte *midnight*
mezzo *medium;*
  middle; half
mezzogiorno *midday*
mi scusi *excuse me*
mia/mie *my (f/f pl)*
miglio (m) *mile*
migliore *better*
minestra (f) *soup*
minestrone (m) *stew*
mini bar (m) *mini bar*
minuto (m) *minute*
mio/miei *my (m/m pl))*
mirtillo (m) *blueberry*
misto/a *mixed*
misura (f) *measure*
moda (f) *fashion*
modulo (m) *form*
moglie (f) *wife*
molti/e *many*
moltissimo *very much*
molto *much; very*
moneta (f) *coin*
montagna (f) *mountain*
monumento (m)
  monument
mora (f) *blackberry*
morbido *soft*
morso (m) *bite*
mossa (f) *move*
moto d'acqua (m) *jet ski*
motocicletta (f) *motorbike*
motore (m) *engine*
mountain bike (f)
  mountain bike
mouse (m) *mouse (computer)*

mozzarella (f)
  mozzarella
mucca (f) *cow*
muffin (m) *muffin*
multa (f) *fine (legal)*
municipio (m) *town hall*
muratore (m) *builder*
muro (m) *wall*
muscoli (m pl) *muscles*
museo (m) *museum*
musica (f) *music*
musica da ballo (f) *dance*
musicista (m) *musician*

N

nascita (f) *birth*
naso (m) *nose*
naturale *natural*
nausea (f) *nausea*
navigare *to navigate*
navigatore satellitare (m)
  satnav
navigazione via satellite
  (f) *satellite navigation*
nebbia (f) *fog*
nebbioso/a *misty*
negozio (m) *shop*
negozio di arredamento (m)
  furniture shop
negozio di articoli da regalo
  (m) *gift shop*
negozio di calzature (m)
  shoe shop
negozio di dischi
  record shop
negozio duty-free (m)
  duty-free shop
neo (m) *mole (medical)*
nero/a *black*
nervosa *nervous*
neve (f) *snow*
niente *anything; nothing*
nightclub (m) *nightclub*

no *no*
noccioline (f pl) *nuts*
noce di cocco (f) *coconut*
noi *us; we*
noleggiare *to hire; to rent*
nome (m) *name*
non *not*
nord (m) *north*
normale *normal*
nostro/nostri/
  nostra/nostre *our*
nota (f) *note*
notte (f) *night*
nove *nine*
novembre *November*
numero (m) *number*
numero del volo (m)
  flight number
numero di conto (m)
  account number
numero di targa (m)
  registration number
numero di telefono (m)
  contact number
nuotare *to swim*
nuoto (m) *swimming*
nuoto subacqueo (m)
  scuba diving
nuovo/a *new*
nuvola (f) *cloud*
nuvoloso/a *cloudy*

O

o *or*
occhiali (m pl) *glasses*
occhiali da sole (m pl)
  sunglasses
occhialini (m pl) *goggles*
occhio (m) *eye*
occupato *engaged/busy*
oceano *ocean*
odiare *to hate*
oggetti di valore (m pl) *valuables*

oggi *today*
ogni *each (every)*
olio (m) *oil*
olio di semi di girasole (m)
  sunflower oil
olio d'oliva (m) *olive oil*
olive (f pl) *olives*
oltre *beyond*
ombrello (m) *umbrella*
ombrellone da spiaggia (m)
  beach umbrella
onda (f) *wave*
online *online*
opaco/a *matt*
opera (f) *opera*
opera teatrale (f) *play*
ora (f) *hour*
orario (m) *timetable*
orario delle visite (m)
  visiting hours
orario di apertura (m)
  opening hours
ordinare *to order*
ordine (m) *order*
orecchino *earrings*
orecchio (m) *ear*
ormeggio (m) *mooring*
oro *gold*
orologio *clock*
orologio da polso (m) *wrist watch*
orribile *awful*
orso *bear*
ospedale (m) *hospital*
ospite (f/m) *guest*
otto *eight*
ottobre *October*
ovest (m) *west*
ovulo *egg*

P

pacchetto (m) *packet*
pacco (m) *parcel*
padella (f) *frying pan*

padre (m) *father*
padrone di casa (m) *host*
paese (m) *country; village*
pagamento (m) *payment*
pagare *to pay*
pagare in contanti *to pay cash*
palcoscenico (m) *stage*
palestra (f) *gym*
paletta (f) *dust pan*
palla (f) *ball*
palla da golf (f) *golf ball*
palla da tennis (f)
  tennis balll
pallina (f) *scoop*
pallone da spiaggia (m)
  beach ball
pallone (m) *football (ball)*
panca (f) *bench*
pancetta (f) *bacon*
pane (m) *bread*
pane nero (m) *brown bread*
pane tostato (m) *toast*
panetteria (f) *baker's*
panificio (m) *bakery*
panne; in panne *broken (in car)*
pannolino (m) *nappy*
pantaloni (m pl) *trousers*
pantofole (f pl) *slippers*
pappa d'avena (f) *porridge*
parabrezza (m) *windscreen*
parare *to save*
parata (f) *block*
paraurti (m) *bumper*
parcheggiare *to park*
parcheggio (m) *parking*
parcheggio per disabili (m)
  disabled parking
parchimetro (m) *parking meter*
parco (m) *park*
parco a tema (m) *theme park*
parco nazionale (m) *national park*
parco safari (m) *safari park*
parenti (m pl) *relatives*

parlare *to speak*
parmigiano (m) *parmesan*
parrucchiere/a (m/f) *hairdresser's*
partecipare *to attend*
partenze (f pl) *departures*
parte posteriore (f) *back*
(*not front of*)
partire *to depart; to leave*
partita (f) *match (sport)*
parto (m) *delivery*
pass per lo ski-lift (m) *lift pass*
passaggio (m) *pass*
passaporto (m) *passport*
passeggero (m) *passenger*
passeggiata (f) *walk*
passo (m) *walk*
pasta (f) *pasta*
paste (f pl) *pastry*
pasticca per la gola (f)
throat lozenge
pasticche antinausea (f pl)
travel-sickness pills
pasticcio (m) *pie*
pastina (f) *bun*
pasto a bordo (m) *flight meal*
patata (f) *potato*
patata dolce (f) *sweet potato*
patatine (f pl) *crisps*
patente di guida (f) *driving licence*
patologia cardiaca (f)
heart condition
pattinaggio su ghiaccio (m)
ice-skating
pattino (m) *skate*
pattumiera (f) *dustbin*
pausa (f) *rest*
pavimento (m) *floor*
paziente (m/f) *patient*
pedaggio (m) *toll*
pedicure (f) *pedicure*
pedina (f) *tile*
peggiore *worse*
pelle (f) *skin*

pellicola (f) *film*
peluche (m) *soft toy*
pendice (f) *slope*
penna (f) *pen*
pensare *to think*
pensione; in pensione *retired*
pensione con colazione (f)
bed and breakfast
pentola (f) *saucepan*
pepe (m) *pepper*
peperoncino (m) *chilli*
per *for*
pera (f) *pear*
perché? *why?*
perdere *to lose*
perdita (f) *leak*
per favore *please*
pericolo *danger*
periferia (f) *suburb*
personale (m) *staff*
persone (f pl) *people*
pesante *heavy*
pesare *to weigh*
pesce (m) *fish*
pesci (m pl) *fish*
pescivendolo (m) *fishmonger*
peso (m) *weight*
pettine (m) *comb*
pezzo (m) *piece*
piacere *to like*
piacevole *nice*
pialla (f) *plane*
pianeta (m) *planet*
piangere *to cry*
pianista (m/f) *pianist*
piantare una tenda
to pitch a tent
piante (f pl) *plants*
piattino (m) *saucer; side plate*
piatto (m) *dish; plate*
piatto principale (m) *main course*
piazza (f) *square (in town)*
piccante *hot (spicy)*

picchetto (m) *tent peg*
piccolo/a *small; little*
picnic (m) *picnic*
piede (m) *foot*
pieno/a *full*
pietra preziosa (f) *stone*
pigiama (m) *pyjamas*
pilates *pilates*
pilota (m/f) *pilot*
PIN (m) *PIN*
pinne (f pl) *flippers*
pinta (f) *pint*
pinzetta (f) *tweezers*
piove *to rain*
piovra (m); **polpo** (m) *octopus*
piscina (f) *swimming pool*
pista ciclabile (f) *cycle lane*
pista da sci (f) *ski slope*
più *more*
piumone (m) *duvet*
pizza (f) *pizza*
platea (f) *stalls*
pneumatico (m) *tyre*
poco *little*
poggiatesta (m) *head rest*
poi *then*
polizia (f) *police*
poliziotta (f) *policewoman*
poliziotto (m) *policeman*
polizza assicurativa (f)
  insurance policy
polizza (f) *policy*
pollame (m) *poultry*
pollice (m) *thumb*
pollo (m) *chicken*
polpette (f pl) *meatballs*
polso (m) *wrist*
polvere (f) *powder*
pomata (f) *ointment*
pomeriggio (m) *afternoon*
pomodoro (m) *tomato*
pomodoro ciliegino (m)
  cherry tomato

pompa (f) *pump*
pompiere (m) *firefighter*
portabagagli (m) *luggage rack*
porta (f) *door*
portafoglio (m) *wallet*
portamonete (m) *purse*
portare *to carry;* **da portar via**
  takeaway
portate (f pl) *courses*
portellone (m) *hatchback*
porticciolo (m) *marina*
porto (m) *harbour*
portone (m) *front door*
porzione (f) *portion*
posacenere (m) *ashtray*
posate (f pl) *cutlery*
possibile *possible*
posta *post*
posta aerea (f) *airmail*
posta in arrivo (f) *inbox*
posteggio dei taxi (m) *taxi rank*
postino (m) *postman*
posto (m) *place; seat*
posto vicino al corridoio (m)
  aisle seat
posto vicino al finestrino (m)
  window seat
potere *can (verb)*
pranzo (m) *lunch*
preferito/a *favourite*
prelevare *to withdraw (money)*
prelievo (m) *withdrawal*
prendere *to take/to catch*
prendere il sole *to sunbathe*
prendere in prestito *to borrow*
prenotare *to book; reserve*
prenotare un volo
  to book a flight
prenotazione (f) *reservation*
preoccupato/a *worried*
preservativo (m) *condom*
pressione arteriosa elevata (f)
  high blood pressure

pressione degli pneumatici (f) *tyre pressure*
prestito (m) *loan*
presto *early; soon*
prezzemolo (m) *parsley*
prezzo (m) *price*
prima di *before*
primato (m) *record*
primavera (f) *spring*
primo/a *first*
primo piano (m) *first floor*
principiante (m/f) *beginner*
profumo (m) *perfume*
proiezione (f) *throw*
prolunga (f) *extension lead*
pronto/a *ready*
pronto soccorso (m) *emergency room*
Pronto Soccorso (m) *accident and emergency*
prossimo/a *next*
provare *to try*
provincia (f) *province*
prugna (f) *plum*
pubblico (m) *audience*
pulire *to wipe*
pulito/a *clean*
pullman (m) *coach*
pullman turistico (m) *tour bus*
pulsante di chiamata (m) *call button*
pungiglione (m) *sting*
punta (f) *tip*
punto (m) *point*

Q

quadrato (m) *square*
qualche volta *sometimes*
qualcosa *anything*
qualcosa *something*
qualcuno/a *somebody*
quale? *which?*

quando? *when?*
quanti/e? *how many?*
quanto? *how much?*
quaranta *forty*
quasi *almost*
quattordici *fourteen*
quattro *four*
quello/a *that*
questo/a *this*
qui *here*
quindici *fifteen*
quindici giorni *fortnight*
quota (f) *altitude*

R

racchetta da tennis (f) *tennis racquet*
racchette da sci (f pl) *ski poles*
radiatore (m) *radiator*
radice (f) *root*
radio (f) *radio*
radio digitale (f) *digital radio*
radiografia (f) *X-ray*
radiosveglia (f) *clock radio*
raffreddore (m) *cold (illness)*
raffreddore da fieno (m) *hay fever*
ragazzo/a (m/f) *boy/girl*
raggio (m) *spoke*
ragno (m) *spider*
rallentare *slow down*
ramo (m) *branch*
rampa di accesso (f) *slip road*
rampa per i disabili (f) *wheelchair ramp*
rapido/a *quick*
raramente *rarely*
rasoio (m) *razor*
rasoio elettrico (m) *electric razor*
rastrelliera (f) *rack*
ratto (m) *rat*
reato (m) *crime*
recinto (m) *fence*
reclamare *to complain*

reffreddore da fieno (m) *hay fever*

regalo (m) *gift; present*

regione (f) *region*

rene (m) *kidney (medical)*

reparto di terapia intensiva (m) *intensive care unit*

repellente per gli insetti (m) *insect repellent*

rete (f) *network*

retro (m) *back (not front of)*

rianimazione (f) *resuscitation*

riavviare *to reboot*

riavvolgimento (m) *rewind*

ribes nero (m) *blackcurrant*

riccio *curly*

ricerca (f) *research*

ricetta medica (f) *prescription*

ricevere *to receive*

ricevuta (f) *bill; receipt*

ricevuta dei bagagli (f) *reclaim tag*

ricezione (f) *reception*

ricordi (m pl) *souvenirs*

ridere *to laugh*

riduzione (f) *reduction*

riempire *to fill*

rilasciare *to release*

rimestare *to stir*

rimorchiare *to tow*

riparare *to fix; repair*

riparazione (f) *repair*

riscaldamento centralizzato (m) *central heating*

riscaldamento (m) *heating*

riscuotere *to cash*

riservare *to reserve*

riso (m) *rice*

riso integrale (m) *brown rice*

rispondere *to answer*

ristorante (m) *restaurant*

ritardo; in ritardo *late*

ritiro bagagli (m) *baggage reclaim*

ritorno (m) *return*

rivelatore di fumo (m) *smoke alarm*

rivista (f) *magazine*

rocce (f pl) *rocks*

rosa *pink*

rosolare *to sauté*

rosso/a *red*

rotaia (f) *rail*

rotatoria (f) *roundabout*

rotondo/a *round*

rotto/a *broken*

rough (m) *rough*

router (f) *router*

rubato/a *stolen*

rubinetto (m) *tap*

rubinetto di arresto (m) *stopcock*

rubino (m) *ruby*

rullino (m) *roll (of film)*

rumoroso *noisy*

ruota (f) *tyre; wheel*

ruota di scorta (f) *spare tyre*

russare *to snore*

S

sabato *Saturday*

sabbia (f) *sand*

sacca da viaggio (f) *holdall*

sacco a pelo (m) *sleeping bag*

sala da pranzo (f) *dining room*

sala d'attesa (f) *waiting room*

sala delle partenze (f) *departure lounge*

salame (m) *salami*

salato *salted*

sale (m) *salt*

salmone (m) *salmon*

salotto (m) *living room*

salsa (f) *sauce*

salute (f) *health*

salvagente (m) *lifebuoy*

salviettina umidificata (f) *wet wipe*

sandali (m pl) *sandals*

sangue dal naso (m) *nosebleed*

sapere *to know (a fact)*

sapone (m) *soap*

sarto (m) *tailor*

sauna (f) *sauna*

sbagliato/a *wrong*

sbarcare *to disembark*

sbucciare *to peel*

sbucciatore (m) *peeler*

scaffale (m) *shelf*

scala (f) *staircase*

scala di sicurezza (f) *fire escape*

scale (f pl) *stairs*

scaricare *to download*

scarpa (f) *shoe*

scarpe (f pl) *shoes*

scarpe da ginnastica (f pl) *trainers*

scarpone (m) *boot*

scarponi (m pl) *walking boots*

scarponi da sci (m pl) *ski boots*

scatola (f) *box*

scatola dei fusibili (f) *fuse box*

scatoletta (f) *can (noun)*

scendere *to get off*

scenografia (f) *set*

scheda del paziente (f) *chart*

scheda di memoria (f) *memory card*

scheggia (f) *splinter*

schiacciata (f) *smash*

schiena (f) *back (body)*

schienale (m) *back*

schiuma da barba (f) *shaving foam*

schizzo (m) *sketch*

sci (m) *skiing*

sci (m pl) *skis*

sciacquare *to rinse*

sciarpa (f) *scarf*

sci d'acqua (m) *water-skiing*

scimmia (f) *monkey*

scivolo (m) *slide*

scodella (f) *bowl*

scogliera (f) *cliff*

scompartimento (m) *compartment*

scopa (f) *brush (cleaning)*

scoperto (m) *overdraft*

scotch (m) *adhesive tape*

scottatura solare (f) *sunburn*

scrivania (f) *desk*

scrivere *to write*

scuola (f) *school*

scuro/a *dark*

scusi *sorry*

secchio (m) *bucket*

secco/a *dry (wine)*

secondo/a *second*

secondo piano (m) *second floor*

sedia a rotelle (f) *wheelchair*

sedia a sdraio (f) *deck chair*

sedia (f) *chair*

seggiolino (m) *child seat*

seggiolone (m) *high chair*

seggiovia (f) *chair lift*

segnale (m) *signal*

segnale stradale (m) *street sign*

segnali stradali (m pl) *road signs*

sei *six*

semaforo (m) *traffic lights*

semi (m pl) *seeds*

seminterrato (m) *basement*

sempre *always*

senape (f) *mustard*

sensibile *sensitive*

sentenza (f) *sentence*

sentiero (m) *footpath*

sentire *to hear*

senza *without*

senza piombo *unleaded*

senza semi *seedless*

separatamente *separately*

sera (f) *evening*

serbatoio (m) *tank*

serpente (m) *snake*

servire *to serve*
servizi (m pl) *services*
servizi di emergenza (m pl)
  emergency services
servizio di babysitting (m)
  babysitting
servizio espresso (m)
  express service
servizio (m) *serve*
seta (f) *silk*
sette *seven*
settembre *September*
settimana (f) *week*
settimana prossima (f) *next week*
settimana scorsa (f) *last week*
shampoo (m) *shampoo*
shock (m) *shock*
sì *yes*
sicuro/a di sé *confident*
sicurezza (f) *security*
sicuro/a *safe*
sigaretta (f) *cigarette*
sigarette (f pl) *cigarettes*
sigaro (m) *cigar*
sinistra (f) *left*
sipario (m) *curtain*
sirena (f) *siren*
sito web (m) *website*
slip (m) *briefs*
smartphone (m) *smartphone*
snowboard (m) *snowboarding*
soda (f) *soda water*
soffitto (m) *ceiling*
soffocare *to choke*
soggiorno (m) *stay*
solamente *only*
soldi (m pl) *money*
sole (m) *sun*
solito/a *usual*
solo/a *alone*
sommare *to add*
sonnifero (m) *sleeping pill*
sopra *above*

sopra *over*
sopracciglio (m) *eyebrow*
sorbetto (m) *sorbet*
sorella (f) *sister*
sorgere del sole (m) *sunrise*
sorpassare *to overtake*
sorpreso/a *surprised*
sorriso (m) *smile*
sostegno (m) *stand*
sottile *thin*
sotto *below; beneath*
sottobicchiere (m) *coaster*
sottopassaggio (m) *underpass*
sottoveste (f) *slip*
souvenir (m) *souvenir*
spalla (f) *shoulder*
spallina (f) *strap*
spartito (m) *score*
spatola (f) *spatula*
spaventato/a *scared*
spazio con fasciatoio (m)
  baby changing facilities
spazzare *to sweep*
spazzola (f) *brush*
spazzolino da denti (m)
  toothbrush
specchio (m) *mirror*
specialità (f) *speciality*
spedire *to send*
spedire la posta *to post*
spegnere *to turn off*
spento/a *off*
spesa (f) *groceries*
spesso *often*
spezie (f pl) *spices*
spiaggia (f) *beach*
spina (f) *plug*
spina dorsale (f) *spine*
spinaci (m pl) *spinach*
spingere *push*
spogliatoio (m) *changing room*
sporco *dirty*
sport (m) *sport*

sport acquatici (m pl) *watersports*
sportello bancomat (m)
  cash machine
sport invernali (m pl)
  winter sports
sposato/a *married*
spray (m) *spray*
spugna (f) *sponge*
spuntino (m) *snack*
squadra (f) *team*
squalo (m) *shark*
stagione (f) *season*
stagioni (f pl) *seasons*
stampa (f) *print (photo)*
stampare *to print*
stanza libera (f) *vacancy (room)*
starnutire *to sneeze*
starnuto (m) *sneeze*
stasera *tonight*
Stati Uniti (m pl) *United States*
statua (f) *statue*
stazione (f) *railway station*
stazione degli autobus (f)
  bus station
stazione di servizio (f)
  petrol station
stazione ferroviaria (f)
  train station
stecca (f) *splint*
step machine (f) *step machine*
sterlina (f) *sterling*
stesso/a *same*
stitichezza (f) *constipation*
stivale (m) *boot*
stomaco (m) *stomach*
stop (m) *stop*
strada (f) *road; street; way*
strade (f pl) *roads*
stress (m) *stress*
stretto/a *tight*
struttura (f) *frame*
studente/studentessa (m/f)
  student

studio (m) *study*
stuzzichini (m pl) *bar snacks*
su *on; over; up*
succedere *to happen*
succo (m) *juice*
succo d'arancia (m) *orange juice*
succo di mela (m) *apple juice*
sud (m) *south*
suo/suoi/sua/sue *his; her*
superficie (f) *area*
supermercato (m) *supermarket*
supporto (m) *support*
supposte (f pl) *suppositories*
surfista (m/f) *windsurfer*
svaligiare *to burgle*
sveglia (f) *alarm clock*
svegliarsi *to wake up (oneself)*
sveglia telefonica (f) *wake-up call*
svenire *to faint*
sviluppare *to develop (film)*

T

tabaccaio (m) *tobacconist*
tabacco (m) *tobacco*
tabellone (m) *notice board*
tachimetro (m) *speedometer*
taglia (f) *size*
tagliaunghie (m) *nail clippers*
tagliere (m) *chopping board*
taglio (m) *cut*
tallone (m) *heel*
tampone (m) *tampon*
tappeto (m) *rug*
tappo (m) *cork*
tardi *late*
tariffa (f) *fare*
tasca (f) *pocket*
tassista (m) *taxi driver*
tasso di cambio (m)
  exchange rate
tastiera (f) *keyboard*
tavola da surf (f) *surfboard*
tavoletta (f) *float*

tavolino (m) *coffee table*
tavolo (m) *table*
taxi (m) *taxi*
tazza (f) *cup*
tazzina da caffè (f) *coffee cup*
teatro (m) *theatre*
teatro dell'opera (m)
   opera house
teglia da forno (f) *baking tray*
teiera (f) *teapot*
telecomando (m) *remote control*
telefonare *to telephone*
telefonata (f) *phone call*
telefono (m) *telephone*
telefono pubblico (m)
   payphone
telegiornale (m) *news*
televisione via cavo (f)
   cable television
televisore (m) *television*
televisore a schermo panoramico
   (m) *widescreen TV*
telo da spiaggia (m)
   beach towel
tè (m) *tea*
tè nero (m) *black tea*
tè verde (m) *green tea*
temperatura (f) *temperature*
tempestoso/a *stormy*
tempo *time*
tempo (m) *weather*
tempo libero (m) *leisure*
tenda (f) *tent*
tenda veneziana (f)
   Venetian blind
tennis (m) *tennis*
tergicristallo (m)
   windscreen wiper
terminal (m) *terminal*
termometro (m) *thermometer*
termostato (m) *thermostat*
terremoto (m) *earthquake*
terreno (m) *soil*

tessuto (m) *fabric*
test di gravidanza (m)
   pregnancy test
testa (f) *head*
testimone (m/f) *witness*
tetto (m) *roof*
thermos (m) *vacuum flask*
tiepido *warm*
tiglio (m) *lime*
timido/a *shy*
timone (m) *oar*
toga (f) *robe*
tonno (m) *tuna*
torace (m) *chest*
torcia (f) *torch*
tornire *to turn*
torsolo (m) *core*
tosse (f) *cough*
tostapane (m) *toaster*
tovagliolo (m) *napkin*
tra *between*
traffico (m) *traffic*
traghetto (m) *ferry*
tram (m) *tram*
tramezzino (m) *sandwich*
tramonto (m) *sunset*
trancio (m) *steak*
trasporti (m pl) *transport*
travellers cheque (m)
   traveller's cheque
tre *three*
treno (m) *train*
trenta *thirty*
treppiede (m) *tripod*
triste *sad*
tritato/a *crushed*
troppo *too*
trota (f) *trout*
trovare *to find*
trucco (m) *make-up*
t-shirt (f) *t-shirt*
tu *you*
tubetto (m) *tube*

tuffarsi *to dive*
turista (m/f) *tourist*
tuta subacquea (f) *wetsuit*
tutti *every*
tutto/i *all*
TV satellitare (f) *satellite TV*

U

uccelli (m pl) *birds*
ufficio *office*
ufficio del turismo (m)
  tourist information office
ufficio di cambio (m)
  bureau de change
**ufficio informazioni turistiche
  (m)** *tourist information*
ufficio oggetti smarriti (m)
  lost property
ufficio postale (m)
  post office
ultimo/a *last*
umido/a *humid*
undici *eleven*
unghia (f) *nail*
uniforme *uniform*
università (f) *university*
uno/a *one*
un poco *a little*
uomo (m) *man*
uragano (m) *hurricane*
urgente *urgent*
usare *to use*
uscita (f) *exit*
uscita di emergenza (f)
  emergency exit
uscita d'imbarco (f)
  boarding gate
utile *useful*

V

vacanza (f) *holiday*
valigetta (f) *briefcase*
valigia (f) *suitcase*

valore (m) *value*
valuta estera (f)
  foreign currency
vasca (f) *bathtub*
vaschetta (f) *tub*
vassoio (m) *tray*
vecchio/a *old*
vedere *to see*
vegetariano/a *vegetarian*
vela (f) *sailing*
veloce *fast; quick*
vendere *to sell*
venerdì *Friday*
venire *to come*
venti *twenty*
ventilatore (m) *fan*
ventoso/a *windy*
veramente *really*
verde *green*
verdura (f) *vegetables*
vero *correct*
versare *to pay in*
verso *towards*
vescica (f) *blister*
vespa (f) *wasp*
veterinario/a (m/f) *vet*
vetro (m) *glass*
via (f) *street; way*
viaggio (m) *travel*
viale (m) *avenue*
vicino *close (near)*
vicino a *beside; by; next to*
videogioco (m) *video game*
vidimare *to validate*
vigneto (m) *vineyard*
villaggio (m) *village*
vincere *to win*
vino (m) *wine*
viola *purple*
violenza carnale (f) *rape*
viottolo (m) *path*
virus (m) *virus*
visita (f) *consultation*

visita guidata (f) *guided tour*
visitatore (m) *visitor*
viso (m) *face*
vista (f) *view*
visto (m) *visa*
vitamine (f pl) *vitamins*
voi *you (pl)*
volante (f) *police car*
volare *to fly*
volere *to want*
volo (m) *flight*
volume (m) *volume*
vomitare *to vomit*
vongola (f) *clam*

W, Y, Z

whisky (m) *whisky*
wifi (m) *Wi-Fi*
wurstel (m) *sausage*

yacht (m) *yacht*
yoga (m) *yoga*
yogurt (m) *yoghurt*
zaino (m) *backpack*
zanzara (f) *mosquito*
zanzariera (f) *mosquito net*
zenzero (m) *ginger*
zero *zero*
zia (f) *aunt*
zio (m) *uncle*
zona (f) *zone*
zoo (m) *zoo*
zucca Butternut (f) *butternut squash*
zucchina (f) *courgette*

ACKNOWLEDGMENTS

ORIGINAL EDITION

Senior Editors Simon Tuite, Angela Wilkes
Editorial Assistant Megan Jones
Senior Art Editor Vicky Short
Art Editor Mandy Earey
Production Editor Phil Sergeant
Production Controller Inderjit Bhullar
Managing Editor Julie Oughton
Managing Art Editor Louise Dick
Art Director Bryn Walls
Associate Publisher Liz Wheeler
Publisher Jonathan Metcalf

Produced for Dorling Kindersley by SP Creative Design
Editor Heather Thomas
Designer Rolando Ugolino
Language content for Dorling Kindersley by First Edition Translations Ltd
Translator Esmerelda Lines
Editor Gabriella Barra
Typesetting Essential Typesetting

Dorling Kindersley would also like to thank the following for their help in the preparation of the original and revised editions of this book: Isabelle Elkaim and Melanie Fitzgerald of First Edition Translations Ltd; Elma Aquino, Mandy Earey, and Meenal Goel for design assistance; Amelia Collins, Nicola Hodgson, Isha Sharma, Janashree Singha, Nishtha Kapil, and Neha Ruth Samuel for editorial assistance; Claire Bowers, Lucy Claxton, and Rose Horridge in the DK Picture Library; Adam Brackenbury, Vânia Cunha, Almudena Diaz, Maria Elia, John Goldsmid, Sonia Pati, Phil Sergeant, and Louise Waller for DTP assistance.

PICTURE CREDITS

The publisher would like to thank the following for their kind permission to reproduce their photographs:

Key: a (above); b (below/bottom); c (centre); l (left); r (right); t (top)

Alamy Images: Alvey & Towers Picture Library p113 cb; PhotoSpin, Inc p38 crb; Tetra Images p20; **Alamy Stock Photo:** Cultura RM p51 br; **Courtesy of Renault:** p26–27 t; **Getty Images:** Reggie Casagrande p148; **PunchStock:** Moodboard p8; **iStockphoto.com:** Mustang_79 p4; **123RF.com:** Cobalt p108 cr; Norman Kin Hang Chan / Bedo p109 clb; Cobalt p134 clb; Cobalt p156 br.

All other images © **Dorling Kindersley**
For further information see: www.dkimages.com

NUMBERS

1 uno *oonoh*	**7** sette *settay*	**13** tredici *traydeechee*	**19** diciannove *deechanovay*	**70** settanta *settanta*
2 due *dooeh*	**8** otto *ottoh*	**14** quattordici *kwattordeechee*	**20** venti *ventee*	**80** ottanta *ottanta*
3 tre *tray*	**9** nove *novay*	**15** quindici *kweendeechee*	**30** trenta *trentah*	**90** novanta *novanta*
4 quattro *kwattroh*	**10** dieci *deeaychee*	**16** sedici *sedeechee*	**40** quaranta *kwarantah*	**100** cento *chentoh*
5 cinque *cheenkway*	**11** undici *oondeechee*	**17** diciasette *deechasettay*	**50** cinquanta *cheenkwantah*	**1,000** mille *meelay*
6 sei *say*	**12** dodici *dodeechee*	**18** diciotto *deechottoh*	**60** sessanta *sessantah*	

ORDINAL NUMBERS

first primo *preemoh*	**fourth** quarto *kwartoh*	**seventh** settimo *setteemoh*	**tenth** decimo *decheemoh*
second secondo *sekondoh*	**fifth** quinto *kweentoh*	**eighth** ottavo *otahvoh*	**twentieth** ventesimo *ventezeemoh*
third terzo *tertsoh*	**sixth** sesto *sestoh*	**ninth** nono *nonoh*	